ENDORSEMENTS

Completing Project Me is a fresh, honest, and biblical approach to what it means to be a follower of Jesus. Matt is transparent and vulnerable in answering some of the toughest questions that life hurls. He has wrestled with the "easy" answers, and through his journey, he takes the reader to greater depths to find God in new ways. This book is more than the popular transactional relationship with God; it calls the reader to a transforming relationship that will last!

—Jo Anne Lyon, ambassador;
general superintendent emerita,
the Wesleyan Church

Whether you're a mature Christian who's looking for something deeper or just starting your spiritual journey, *Completing Project Me* is the read you've been waiting for. Matt's book is filled with frequently overlooked biblical concepts and coupled with powerfully illustrated stories that flow from a fruitful ministry career. Read it with a commitment to prayerful introspection. The teachings provide a path for growing into a more complete you as one designed by God.

—Dr. Stephen Fitch,
founder and CEO of
Eden Reforestation Projects

Completing
Project
ME

How Understanding
God's Perspective
Changes Yours

MATTHEW A. THOMAS

BroadStreet
PUBLISHING

BroadStreet Publishing® Group, LLC
Savage, Minnesota, USA
BroadStreetPublishing.com

Completing Project Me: How Understanding God's Perspective
Changes Yours

Stock or custom editions of BroadStreet Publishing titles may be
purchased in bulk for educational, business, ministry, fundraising,
or sales promotional use. For information, please email info@
broadstreetpublishing.com.

Cover and interior by Garborg Design at GarborgDesign.com

Printed in United States of America
19 20 21 22 23 5 4 3 2 1

CONTENTS

Foreword

By Gerald L. Sittser

I teach at a university, and every so often a student says to me, "I want to be a writer." I always appreciate hearing such an aspiration. In the course of the conversation, I always ask what it is they want to write about. Students often don't know how to answer this question. They aren't yet sure about what they care about most deeply and what they consider true and good and beautiful.

Matt Thomas is different. Matt is mature and experienced. He is a visionary leader, church planter, and missionary statesman. For the past twelve years, he has served as bishop of the Free Methodist Church and presided during a period of massive growth. I am quite certain Matt never aspired to be a writer when he was a student; he is too much of an entrepreneur. But now nearing retirement, he certainly has something to write about, and in *Completing Project Me*, he writes it well.

Matt moved to Spokane, Washington, to plant a church. Timberview, as it was named, met for worship during its early years in the chapel at Whitworth University, where I serve as a professor. It was only natural for the two of us to bump into each other, which led to an occasional cup of coffee. Eventually, we launched a reading group for ten senior pastors in town. We read mostly classics. In fact, we never read a book that was less than 500 years old! I discovered early on that Matt is smart. He is a reader and a thinker, but he is first and foremost a preacher and a pastor.

No group lasts forever, of course. We met monthly for some five years. Then Matt began to tell us about an invitation he had received from the Free Methodist Church to serve as a bishop. He eventually accepted the invitation, which, due to his travel schedule, forced him to withdraw from the group. We maintained communication, and when we met, he would regale me with stories of his travels as bishop. He reported that God is at work around the world, and it was thrilling to learn how.

In the fall of 2018, we had our annual cup of coffee. He told me he was writing a book that he had been thinking about for a long time. After reading it, I realized that he had been thinking about it his whole life. *Completing Project Me* reflects Matt's deep understanding of what it means to be a follower of Jesus. This book contains deep insights, to be sure, but its primary value is in calling us to Jesus Christ as the way *to* life and *of* life.

Matt knows, loves, and trusts God. He knows faith does not grow by trying to muster more of itself. Faith grows when it looks away from self to focus on the only One who is worthy of faith. The book is about "completing project me," but the one who does the completing is the One who, beginning a good work in us, promises to bring it to completion.

This book is also full of practical and personal wisdom. It is concrete, accessible, and draws on Matt's many years of personal experiences and careful study of the Bible. I learned more about his family, his ministry, and his travels. I learned about the "saints" he has known and worked with around the world and the global church—both her trials and triumphs. This book has an aura of "real life" about it.

Matt knows how to write simply and clearly. Certain phrases and images still ring in my ear: "*pleroma,*" "smaller things," "least likely places," "relational prayer," "shining things," "recycling," "look through and beyond." He turns just the right phrase and captures a truth with just the right image.

I teach and write about the church fathers and mothers, especially from the early Christian period—people like Basil of Caesarea and Macrina the Younger. The church has benefitted from these great Christians throughout her history. I consider Matt Thomas a church father. He is a man of faith and goodness. He lives well and loves well, not only when in the view of the public but also at home. He is a man of influence, not because of a big personality or an abundance of wealth but because of his walk with Christ. This book is the fruit of a life of discipleship. It will enlarge your vision of God and your view of the Christian life. More than that, it will inspire you to live the Christian life. It certainly inspired me.

Gerald L. Sittser, PhD
Professor of Theology, Whitworth University
Author of *A Grace Disguised, The Will of God as a Way of Life*,
and *Water from a Deep Well*

The Biggest Project of Your Life

We know what projects are. Projects involve an idea or assignment to make something new or to solve a problem. We have done them in school, at work, and at home. Sometimes the raw materials to complete them are in our possession. Sometimes we need to create or purchase the materials. But when a project is done well, we have a sense of satisfaction and accomplishment.

Your life is a project. Whether you know it or not, you were born with all the necessary raw materials as a glorious creation of God. But something happened in history that set us all back. The pesky sin problem clouded our vision of what we could become, dulled our hopes, and destroyed our ability to do life on our own. Yet the raw materials still exist, and God is the one who has set out to remake us into what we were intended to be. He promised to do that, but he requires our full participation to complete the work. This is the biggest project of your life—the completion of you. God is interested in it. It should be the project that interests you the most and of which you are eager to complete. This book is about that promise and process.

As with any project, it is a journey. It is not completed in a moment, however; there are significant moments and decisions along the way, without which we would never be complete. The apostle Paul admitted he was still finding his way even though he had been many places, accomplished many things, and performed many miracles. He said, "Not that I have already obtained all this, or have already been made perfect, but I press on to take hold of that for which Christ Jesus took hold of me" (Philippians 3:12). He admitted that the project was underway but not complete. He also promised to continue moving forward until it was. We should all be keenly interested in what God is doing for us and in us. We should also be deeply committed to understand what God is up to and how we should respond.

Do not view your life as a compilation of meaningless or useless events. View the whole of your experiences and relationships as valuable parts of the project. This book will help you see how God works and recognize the patterns that unfold as he remakes us into the people we were meant to be. It is my hope that you will look at everything, not just the monumental events in life, as part of the project. I hope you will come to understand that sometimes the smallest and most mundane things in life make the biggest impact and contribute the most to our development.

All of us intuitively ask the larger *why* question of purpose when the larger events in life occur—the death of a family member, the loss of a job, a critical move that impacts the whole family, or a serious illness. The bigger the issue, the bigger and more pronounced the questions. Most of us, however, do not ask either the larger *why* question or the more mundane *what, where, when, how,* or *who* questions when the small events in life occur—meeting a unique person at lunch, obtaining a bonus at work, a minor physical setback, an inconvenient detour en route to work, being stood up for a lunch appointment, or having either a very good or very bad evaluation at work or school. It is possible that we aren't asking the right questions about the big things in life because we are unpracticed at asking questions about the smaller things in life. When we are practiced at seeing everything as part of the project, we start asking more productive questions and making observations and looking for God to work along the way. When we are unaccustomed to being attentive to the small things, we will most certainly be confused in the larger things. Most people are. We will take a look at all of it. It is my hope that you will better understand God's heart, perspective, and ways of working. It is also my hope that you will learn to appreciate and respond to what he is doing and wants to do in you.

After each chapter you will find a section called "Project Me." Here you will find opportunities to reflect, pray, write, and take other steps toward better understanding and advancing in God's work in your life.

Now, let's enter into project you!

PART I

A Biblical View of Fullness

Completion Is the Goal

I generally finish what I start. I wanted to play saxophone in the school band from a young age. Fifth grade was the first year of band in our school. My father said he would buy a saxophone if I would commit to playing it all the way through high school. He said, "I won't contribute to helping you start what you can't finish." I said that I would, so he bought the saxophone. And I held up my end of the bargain. I heard him say many times, regarding relational, athletic, or work commitments, "Don't start unless you are committed to finish." For the most part that describes my life. However, there have been moments when I started well but failed to finish. I am not likely the only one to have unfinished pursuits in some area of life.

One of the most glaring memories of not finishing what I had started was when I competed in track and field. I was a modestly good distance runner as a teen. In my early years of track and field, I finished most of my races in the top three, winning a fair share of them. When I was sixteen years old, in a statewide meet I qualified for a regional event in the two-mile run where the top two finishers would then qualify for a national event. The national event would be on the East Coast, and I lived on the West Coast. I really wanted to see the country and compete against the best runners in the nation.

The regional qualifying race began at 2:00 p.m. on a day in early August. It was 102 degrees on the track at the start of the race. About sixteen runners had qualified for this event from three states. Four decided not to compete due to the heat. I thought that only increased my chances of winning. The gun sounded, and after about two of the eight laps I found myself in second place. Not bad. I held that position for two more laps. Then something happened that I had never experienced before. I think I was experiencing heat stroke. My teenage vocabulary was less medical. We called it "bonking." And I bonked hard. With only two of the eight laps remaining, I did something I'd never done before, and never did afterward, at a track event. I walked off the track. I fell on the infield grass. I did not finish. For some reason, I remember that race with more graphic detail than every race I won.

Most of the time, I am able to finish what I start. Sometimes, as with all people, I have not been able to finish well or at all. You likely understand. Most of us experience failure at one time or another. Sometimes lack of commitment or excitement does us in. Sometimes hitting our limits or overpromising lead to quitting early. Sometimes we just get tired, distracted, or have other more important things that take precedence. We are only human. And that's the point. Humans fail though they desperately want to succeed.

But God is different. He never started anything he did not finish or is in process even now of finishing. From the beginning of the Bible until the end of it, God famously starts things and completes them. Genesis 1:1 begins, "In the beginning God created the heavens and the earth." Then, after a chapter filled with detailed descriptions about both the order of creation and the roles and limits he granted creation, Genesis 2:1 says, "Thus the heavens and the earth were created in all their vast array." This is a statement dripping with starting and finishing what is started. God started it, and he completed it. He finished what he started with all of the goodness he pours into everything.

How God worked in the creation is the pattern for everything that follows. The whole Bible is full of God starting and finishing. In fact, after he completed that initial work, he rested (Genesis 2:2–3). We certainly do not believe that God needed rest. He is not susceptible to physical weariness or exhaustion. Yet he rested anyway. Many would say that he was setting an example for us to follow. Resting found its way in the middle of the Ten Commandments telling us how we should live. The fifth commandment has more words than most of the other commandments put together. He commanded it because he knew we needed it on multiple levels.

God himself did not need rest. He simply did it. It could be that his rest was nothing more than an example for us to follow. He certainly did not need it. Perhaps he rested for his own enjoyment. It may have served as a pause; a pause that signaled a break before resuming more activity, before the next phase of his plan, indicating that more was to come. Or perhaps he rested to note that he had completed something. If that is the case, it's no wonder that resting would be part of God's rhythm. He is constantly finishing things—fulfilling promises, getting people to safe places, performing miracles that overcome obstacles, and fixing human messes.

After that creation event, humanity fell from relationship with God and his design for them. They fell hard. Still, before he got very far from the start, he made the appropriate adjustment to the colossal human collapse and reiterated to Noah what he said before to Adam: "Be fruitful and increase" (Genesis 9:1, 7). In short, God was bound and determined to finish what he started regardless of human failing. He wanted to get back on track. He does not quit though we sometimes do. He will not fail. He is sure to succeed.

And that is how it goes throughout the pages of Scripture. God has completion in mind before he starts anything. Consider the prophets themselves. They are evidence that God continues the theme of finishing what he starts. The prophets were assigned words from God to share with the people. Sometimes the prophets affirmed the people with words from God, but most often they spoke corrective words to the people, telling of the consequences for disobedience or bad behavior. In the case of the latter, the prophets' words contained several elements.

First, the prophets conveyed God's thoughts about the current condition of a specific person or society in general. Usually that behavior was bad; hence, they needed the prophecy. The prophets would tell the people that God saw their hearts and knew what they were up to, which was usually unacceptable.

Nathan was a prophet during King David's time. He knew what David was up to: an affair, a conniving coverup, and ultimately a murder (2 Samuel 11). David was God's man, but he could not be God's man like that, so God had Nathan call David out (12:1–12). Nothing gets better by adding foolishness to foolishness, which David was doing. Of course, Nathan did what any good prophet would do—reveal the nonsense to stop the charade. Prophets spoke truth to people and confronted sin. That is what they did the most. And it was always to stop something that was impeding the person from achieving what God wanted to achieve through them.

Second, prophets would typically convey the consequences that would result from bad behavior. Often, the prophet would relay (quite specifically) what God was going to do if the people did not stop their bad behavior. Sometimes these consequences included the people being dispossessed of their land or possessions; other times the consequences took the form of invading nations, pestilence, drought, or something leading to death or injury. Sometimes it included all of the above (see

Habakkuk). That part of the prophets' job never endeared them to the kings or wealthy and powerful individuals of their day.

Jeremiah was successful in God's eyes as a prophet because he spelled out consequences to kings and the whole nation of Israel, but he was nothing more than a nuisance to the societal elites. Despite being arrested, abused, and jeered, he didn't stop telling them what would happen. At one point, the leaders were so exasperated with Jeremiah that they threw him in prison (Jeremiah 37). Their frustration later escalated, and he was thrown in a cistern (38:1–6). In both cases, they wanted him out of sight, out of mind. Having someone constantly warning you about your failure is bad enough. It is worse when people like Jeremiah tell others what horrible things will happen if you persist. But, again, that's what biblical prophets did.

That brings us to the third responsibility of the prophets: spreading hope. They frequently closed their messages with some good news. They revealed what God would do to fix, restore, or complete the work that had been delayed because of the people's disobedience. The prophets were reminders that people fail but God does not. People fail to finish but God always does. He never gives up on a promise or commitment. This is the prophets' message that we like the most. Hope is in it because God promises to continue working. Examples are found and often quoted from passages like Isaiah 55, Ezekiel 37, and Jeremiah 33, since the happy resolution part of the prophets' words are welcomed by everyone who reads them today. After all, who doesn't like a happy ending? We like God's commitment to complete his work.

Those chapters, and others like them, promise us new hearts, the rebirth of a nation, descendants who will have it better than their parents, and God's continued presence. Through prophets like these, we hear about nations rejoicing, mountains dripping with new wine, sickness being a thing of the past, lions and lambs getting along as friends, and the hungry being satisfied. Of all the words of the prophets, these are the words that make us smile. We feel that justice will be served. The downcast will be lifted up. Hurts will be healed. Troubles that have plagued so many people for so long will go away.

With the prophets, we circle back to the point that God will finish what he started. In the creation, he got things started with a promise to complete it all. Through the prophets, God acknowledged how things went awry with creation, he warned folks to get back on track or suffer the consequences, and he reminded us that he will finish what he started and fulfill his promises well. It is as though he had the creation and the culmination of history in mind when he gave words to the prophets. The prophets remind us that God has not forgotten us or let our misery escape his attention. Their prophecies bring the message of God's steadfastness full circle to God finishing what he promised and started. He will always deliver.

God is a God who completes what he sets out to do. He is a finisher. That theme reverberates through the Psalms. Consider Psalm 37. In this psalm, King David encouraged the reader to neither fear nor envy evil people (v. 1). Instead, he went on to tell people to trust in God and wait patiently for him (vv. 3–7). He reminded us that God will settle the score (vv. 9–11). He testified that he knows what he's talking about since he has been around a while and has seen not only quite a bit of misery but also the faithfulness of God (v. 25). Hang in there (v. 34). In the end, God will work things out (vv. 35–40). Why? Because God completes what he started.

There are other psalms where the writer is expecting God to finish things, only differently. Many of the psalms fully hope and expect that the bad people will "get theirs" in the end. They are counting on God to settle the score, not leaving evil unpunished. Their hope in these psalms is that God will finish off those who are bringing trouble upon the innocent or taking advantage of the weak. Psalms 10, 55, 56, and 79 are pleas to the Lord to do something about those who gleefully cause pain in others. The flavor of these psalms seems to be in stark contrast to the more encouraging ones. The basic hope and confidence in both the psalms filled with trouble and the psalms filled with encouragement are that God will finish things well. That is the link between the psalms that seem aggressive and the ones that are warm and comforting. God will complete what he set out to do. He is not going to leave things as they are. Suspense is temporary. Resolution is coming.

That is why the Psalms bring so much comfort to those who are in distress. For those who have experienced hardship, this collection of poems and songs are encouraging words from people who hung in there, written for people finding it hard to hang in there. The psalmists are wise and experienced people. They might not be prophets. But just as the prophets told a bigger story leading up to God's finishing work in the nations, the psalmists tell personal stories about God's finishing work in individuals and nations.

Older, oppressed, abused, and weary people love, read often, memorize, and quote the Psalms perhaps more than any other book of the Bible. Why? It is not really because of the poetic nature of the writing. The Psalms resonate with those whose lives have been seasoned with difficulty and occasional tragedy. Those who experience hardship but remain faithful to God resonate with the psalmists' who have found that, even in the darkest moments, they could rely upon the one who follows through, brings justice, prepares good, protects the fragile, and answers prayer. God will finish what he started. Don't become discouraged. That is the general message of the Psalms.

Our family experienced several difficulties through the years. I have served as a pastor, regional leader, global church leader, teacher, college president, and missionary, among other things. The overwhelming outcome of all of that has been a life of privilege and joy. Each member of my immediate family is wonderful, mature, and impactful to a high degree in their respective settings. Their vocations are honorable, and they have collected more than their share of awards and accolades.

My wife, Marlene, is a joy to all who know her and one of the most loving people I know. We have always delightfully partnered together throughout the decades of ministry we have been privileged to share.

But anyone who has led anything worth leading, and with results worth celebrating, knows that, if you put yourself in positions of leadership, you will experience not only blessings but also expose yourself to challenges. There will likely be people who oppose your efforts. In that sense, I am not an exceptional leader. We have had joys uncontainable but often celebrated, but we have had challenges that would have not come if we were not in positions of leadership or taking stands that threatened evil. I have had attempts on my life, experienced legal threats, and had my character maligned by those who were motivated by greed or fear. I was briefly kidnapped. We were robbed and faced extortion attempts. Admittedly, these negative experiences have been the exception rather than the rule.

One difficulty stands out above all others since it was a tragedy that is every parent's worst fear—the death of a child. We have four outstanding children: Luke, Mitchell, Samuel, and Charese. They are adults with families of their own. All of them are leaders in their careers and communities. All of them are fruitful people and admired by those who know them. They all have exceptional character and skill. We are proud of them in the healthiest ways. But we all shared the same tragically significant loss as a family.

After seventeen months of aggressive cancer, Mitchell (our son, who was a youth pastor), succumbed to his mortality just five days after his twenty-eighth birthday. He lived an exemplary, faith-filled life. He loved everyone and was loved by everyone with whom I have ever spoken. He was wise beyond his years. He had rock-solid faith in God and held on to hope tenaciously until his final breaths. In those days, he yielded to the possibility of leaving his wife and the rest of us to be with God forever, though his preference was clearly to remain and continue ministry, have a family, and reap more fruit from his labors.

We all walked that journey with him for about a year and a half. His brother, Sam, was by his side much of the time since they lived and ministered together in the same city. Though we journeyed with him, Marlene was with him the bulk of those seventeen months, not leaving his side for the final four months before he moved on. We prayed earnestly for his healing. We sought the Lord with tears. We wanted God to do something to undo this plague of sickness. We prayed, loved, laughed, sang, and cried together. And we read the Psalms often and with more connection and understanding than ever before. Psalms 23, 27, 34, and 91 were Mitch's favorites. Why did we find solace in the Psalms? Certainly because of our ability to identify with the psalmists and receive comfort from their words. We found comfort mostly because we knew that God would not leave our pain and difficulty unresolved. There would be temporary healing here on earth, or permanent healing and rest in heaven. We knew that not even death has the final word. God would bring a good ending to this tragedy wherever it landed Mitch.

Because of Mitch's confidence that came from knowing that God has the final word, his outlook was very different than that of his fellow sufferers on the oncology ward, most of whom had "fixable" cancer while he did not. He continued to meet with many of them and share the hope he had in a loving and caring manner. Even the doctors and nurses told us his engagement, hope, and joy were remarkable. One doctor said to me, "I have been working on this ward for two decades, and I have never seen anyone like your son." When patients saw he was laboring in his last days, they all were asking about him with unusual interest. Each one of them had a story about how he touched them and impacted their lives. It was an interesting community.

On one of Mitch's better days, I told him about the love and care expressed from both the patients and the healers on the ward. I told him how deeply appreciated he was. I mentioned that several people wondered how he could have the energy and love to minister to them even though his condition was the worst on the ward. So, I asked him, "Mitch, people want to know how you are able to care for others despite your own sickness. They want to know what the difference is in you." He replied:

> God has done this. And walking in his love, forgiveness, and holiness matters. Yes, holiness matters. I have no regrets, no moral issues to settle, no relationships to repair, no decisions to undo, and no priorities to rearrange. My heart is clear. My memories are sweet. My relationships are outstanding. My ministry has been rewarding. My Jesus is always near. My hope is in the Lord, and I know I will be with him someday. I am just fighting a physical illness while experiencing the riches of God in every other way. Walking in the Spirit and allowing the Spirit to walk in me is living in holiness. I have illness—that's all. If I carried spiritual sickness, lacked forgiveness, harbored bitterness, lacked purpose, or carried regret, the illness would be unbearable. I have none of that. It pays to be clean. Then, when pain comes, it stands alone with little force behind its punch. For me, everything that is not pain is peace. Peace is a wonderful fruit of holiness.

He spoke those words in his final week. In them, he was telling a story of completion even though there were still a few miles left to be traveled on the journey. He knew that God is a finisher and would complete what needed to be completed in us here. He knew that God would finish what needed to be completed beyond the momentary experience. Mitch was simply conveying what the psalmists wrote over and over again.

The message of completion does not end with the Psalms. It continues to resonate throughout the New Testament. Jesus came and lived a powerful life. He spoke powerful words. He did an unparalleled work on the cross that led to the salvation of all who would believe in him. And, consistent with what we read in the Old Testament, Jesus completed his work. In fact, among the few things he said from the cross, Jesus said, "It is finished" (John 19:30). His work was done. No threads of work remained undone. Through Jesus, God could do whatever needed to be done for anyone at any time in history. Jesus' completed work made possible the completion of all God's work in us.

Even the words and works of Jesus, complete as they were, do not end the New Testament's story of God's ability to finish what he starts. The Bible ends with the book Revelation—not just an example of God finishing things. It is a book that describes how God finishes everything. The picture is awesome. And even though it is a little opaque in some sense, it is abundantly clear that God is in charge, has the final words, and resolves everything. That is finishing with an exclamation point!

However, there are many hints in the New Testament about the grand spectacle of Revelation that personalize God's finishing ability. God does not just complete what he started in the world; he completes us. The apostle Paul wrote a letter to the church in Philippi. After a very brief introduction, he thanked them and told them how he was praying for them. He called them partners in this most important journey. Then he said something that demonstrated his own understanding of the Scriptures from beginning to end: "Being confident of this, that he who began a good work in you will carry it on to completion until the day of Christ Jesus" (Philippians 1:6). As with the creation story, the words of the prophets, the confidence of the psalmists, and the story known to his contemporaries, though yet unspoken (Revelation), Paul knew that whatever God started, he would complete.

Those words, as he told his friends, are not just a cosmic reality but a personal one. He told the Philippians that God started a work in them and would finish it. With his knowledge of Scripture in mind, Paul could say with certainty that if God started this work he would also be faithful to complete it. Whatever that work was that God had started, it would be completed—if for no other reason than God started it, and he finishes what he starts. God completes all projects he starts.

Paul knew, however, that it would require our obedience and tenacity to carry on in faith with the Lord. He said to those same people that he was not perfect yet. He said, "Not that I have already obtained all this or have already been made perfect, but I press on to take hold of that for which Christ Jesus took hold of me" (Philippians 3:12). He understood that this project God was working on comes with the expectation that we let God do his work while obediently doing the work that he calls us to do. God is perfecting. We are pressing on. We simply cannot be passive in the process, yet with confidence we know that whatever we need to take hold of, he has taken hold of us. We can know that God will grant us strength to do what needs to be done as we march closer to the finish line (Philippians 3:13–14).

The good work that God began in the Philippians is the same good work he begins in those who receive him, surrender to him, and choose to follow him. God invests in the good work he starts, and he fully expects us to press on in completing this project. He expects us to have faith in him and follow him obediently. Hence, just as Paul could be quite confident that God would complete his work in the Philippians, we can be just as confident that God will complete his work in us. He will do everything that needs to be done to complete this project of his, which is "me." He will do the heavy lifting. I must learn and follow as he teaches and leads.

So, how do I connect this very intentional involvement of God we see in the Bible with my life? Everything he starts in the Bible he seems to finish (or we can at least see where he is headed). How will the seemingly haphazard and disconnected events in my life contribute to my finished product? That is what we'll continue exploring.

Project Me

- Think about a time you were unable to finish an important task (a competition, an important work project, or even a promise you made to a friend). In reflecting upon that time, how did it make you feel? Do you still feel disappointment? Spend time praying with an accountability partner about this. Allow God to heal you, and allow yourself to feel his forgiveness.

- What is your favorite Bible passage about God finishing what looked to be unlikely? Write in your journal some of the reasons it resonates with you.

- Mitch had great confidence, despite his grim chances of recovery. Who do you know like Mitch? Reflect on some of their attributes. How can you be more like them in your daily life?

2

How Many Layers Are There?

Most people are living only for the here and now, but the here and now is not very expansive. Many think their immediate experience is all there is to life. However, we should remember that we are living in the light of eternity. There is more than just what we can see and experience.

It is said that for every action, there is an equal and opposite reaction. A popular example of this is a Newton's cradle, where the force of one little ball, suspended in a row of several other balls, triggers a rhythmic back and forth motion when it is pulled back and released. One ball hits the others, and back and forth they will go for quite some time. That is the equal and opposite reaction. It works that way when speaking of inanimate objects of all kinds. The laws of mathematics are in place dealing with speed and mass leading to force. The problem is that this is not the case with human beings. There is much more to every action. There are innumerable reactions to every action. In fact, every human action entails a stream of reactions, consequences, and influences. Herein lies the problem: Many people think that whatever they do will only have a single consequence. Those folks could not be more mistaken.

Consider a single person in line at a drive-through window who pays it forward. The person may simply be intending to bless the person in the car behind them. Or they may think that their generosity might prompt the same in the driver behind them to do the same for the person in the car behind them. And it may be that their generosity does just that. However, sometimes an act of generosity can have implications for hours, days, weeks, years, and even a lifetime. It happened to me one day when I went to pay for my coffee at a drive-through window. According to Adele, the young woman taking payments, it had been going on for two days.

One act of valor can inspire a generation of people to do the same. One person's life-changing decision can break a multigenerational cycle of violence or crime for succeeding generations. One commitment to do the right thing can lead to scores of people being saved from illness, abuse, and death. It happens all the time. Stories abound. You likely know some. You may be an example of how a single act of good has surprised you in the grand scope of its impact. In reality, this happens every day. Whether the results are heroic and inspiring or mundane, your actions have more than one consequence.

The same is true for the opposite end of the spectrum. Acts of sin, injustice, and abuse have consequences and effects that can sometimes roll on for generations. I believe every person who has ever done something wrong has at one time or another thought in a calculating way: *Why not? The only thing that can or will happen will be ...,* or *It is not going to make that much difference. The worst thing that can happen is ...* The very thought behind those statements is an error of the greatest order—one that caused millions of people to think, at a later point, *If I only knew at the time that it would lead to this, I never would have done it.* The initial thought is that there will only be one contained, equal and opposite consequence associated with an action. The outcome is the horror of a lifetime of disappointment, addiction, failure, hurt, or pain.

That kind of statement does not just come from someone who has had an affair, thinking that cheating one time will not impact their marriage. Neither does it come only from people with addictive personalities, thinking that the first drink or first hit will not matter much. Unintended consequences can consume anyone who does anything that violates their conscience, compromises their commitments, breaks their trustworthiness, or negatively impacts another person. There may be an equal and opposite reaction to every action when it comes to a Newton's cradle or balls on a pool table. But there is an amplified response to every action when it comes to what people do and say in the everyday world. That is just the way it is.

In fact, the Bible is replete with examples of amplified impact from beginning to end. One person takes a bite from an apple, thinking this would be good food for a moment, but that short-term indulgence negatively impacts every child born thereafter. Another person hangs on a cross and opens the door of hope for an eternity for all who have ever lived who respond by faith. Whether good or bad, there is more to everything than what we can see. The implications run further than the action itself.

There is a Greek word in the Bible that gives flesh to this concept: *pleroma*. It means "fullness that extends beyond the momentary experience" or "promised fulfillment." Filling a glass to the top is *full*. Filling it so that it never runs dry is *pleroma*. The word implies that whatever has happened will be more complete down the road than it is now. It is used in the Bible, for the most part, in instances where God does something that continues to grow or impact in greater ways as history unfolds than what the people impacted by the event or action think. In Romans 13:10, the use of *pleroma* indicates that, according to God's law, every good thing we hoped to get out of living is truly completed when we live in love. And living in love leads us to live out God's law. Further, living in love takes us beyond living out God's law. It results in making it possible to do everything well and with the right motives. *Pleroma* means that whatever you think the outcome is, or should be, to anything (good or bad), there is more than what you expect. There are more consequences, more people impacted, more results, and more influences upon you than you first believed. It means that when we think the effect of something is over, it might just be getting started.

Even where that word is not used, the concept of *pleroma* is prevalent throughout the Bible. Jesus implied it when he spoke with a woman near a well. She went to the well to get water. Drinking that water would momentarily satisfy her thirst for an hour or two on a hot day. He talked about taking a drink of water that would allow a person to never thirst again (John 4:14; 7:37–38). Jesus implied that he was offering something far different and far more sustaining than momentary, physical satisfaction. He indicated that taking a drink from him would sustain a person for life.

The word *pleroma* emerges powerfully in the Bible to describe how fully Jesus represents God, though he just appeared as a man: "For God was pleased to have all his fullness [*pleroma*] dwell in him" (Colossians 1:19). And more descriptively: "For in Christ all the fullness [*pleroma*] of deity lives in bodily form" (Colossians 2:9). It looks from the outward appearance that Jesus represents God by making wise statements and healing many who needed healing. However, in reality, that was just the beginning. That was never intended to be the full expression of his deity. There is something much more powerful, eternal, and transformational in who Jesus is and what he can do. He did not come to heal a few illnesses and speak a few words of wisdom. He came to change the world and give all who believe in him access to salvation now and eternity to come. That is why he came (John 10:10). Jesus embodied more of God than people realized. In fact, he was God more than people realized. And God the Father used Jesus more than people realized. Who Jesus is and what he was (and is) up to was far more than meets the eye.

His impact upon the world is more than anyone in his day could have imagined. His work continued long after the apostles died. He is still at work. And his work is still working. That's *pleroma*.

Interestingly, the Bible references the word *pleroma* in the context of the church, people, and events. Colossians 2:10 uses the word, saying, "And you have been given fullness [*pleroma*] in Christ." Paul's letter to the Colossians continues, informing people how they are more and can become more than what they were or could muster on their own. The bulk of chapters 3 and 4 speak about a life that is lived beyond a person's will and strength. The rest of his letter explains in detail how by coming to Christ and living by faith in him, they can do more, live better, understand more, and have better motives than they think possible. In other words, even though they were Christians when he wrote them, he was telling them that there's more.

The church itself is a mystery in this sense. When we think of church, we might think of a group of people who gather together in a brick building on the corner of First and Main on Sunday morning to have a pre-service chat, eat some donuts, drink coffee, sing some songs, listen to a sermon, and have a little fellowship afterward in the fellowship hall. God has more in mind for the church. In fact, he created and sees the church as a collection of redeemed people, empowered by the Holy Spirit to represent God on earth and living in love and forgiveness, who have experienced and understand God's grace. God launched the church to impact the world indelibly for him. The apostle Paul said it this way in Ephesians 1:22–23: "God placed all things under his feet and appointed him to be head over everything for the church, which is his body, the fullness [*pleroma*] of him [Jesus] who fills everything in every way."

That is powerful stuff. God has all of his fullness rest in Jesus. Jesus puts his fullness in the church, making it far more powerful and impactful than people realize. Even those who heard him preach to the masses and saw his miracles did not understand that he was building a community of people who would have his fullness even after he was gone. With those words in Ephesians, we realize that the church is more than what we see on Sunday morning. The church universal is Jesus' family on earth, empowered to live a transformational life and filled with his Spirit to do extraordinary things and be extraordinary people. The local church with God at its center represents more and has more potential to be used of God than most people see. The church is the fullness of Jesus. Let that sink in for a moment the next time you are with your friends in the foyer. Mull that over with your Bible study mates. The potential of you and your friends doing something in Jesus Christ that you cannot do alone is mind-boggling.

I remember being in a worship service at a crowded and simply constructed church in the Sidama highlands of Ethiopia. The town was within walking distance of Arbegona, a small town in its own right. The service started conventionally with singing and praising God, which is a common beginning in church services around the world. Some congregants danced to the music, adding cultural flare, which I appreciated. It was joyful movement to music that was delightful to watch. I was with my friend, Steve Fitch, who is the founding director of Eden Reforestation Projects, a hugely successful creation care organization that plants trees and, in the process, restores God's creation, offers jobs, and saves lives. He was well-known and loved by all there. As Steve's guest, I was invited to speak. But, before I was very much into the message, there was a disturbance. It was not just noise. There was a palpable presence of evil. The people of God gathered around some others who were not people of faith. The love of God in the presence of his people overwhelmed the evil that was present, and the moment changed from one that could only be described as chilling to one of indescribable peace and joy. That transition was instantaneous. The fullness of the church was on display because the fullness of Jesus, who filled the church with his Spirit, was present.

We all have fullness (*pleroma*) who are in Christ (Ephesians

3:19). There is something more than meets the eye for those who are "in Christ," as the Bible states repeatedly. I cannot begin to recount all the times I have done something or said something that had powerful impact upon people while I was totally unaware of what God was doing. God was at work when we were not even aware. We think our words only result in the outcomes we intend for them. In reality, God takes our simple words and actions and reserves the right to use them in ways that transcend our own understanding.

I remember preaching a sermon once about the love of God for all of us. Every verse I used in the Bible really addressed one thing—the love of God. I spoke about all the implications of God's love for us. I do not think I used the word "faith" once in my message. If I did, it was not intentional. I did not explore the concepts of faith or even talk about how love relates to faith, despite the many verses that make this connection. There was nothing in my message about faith at all. I assumed my audience had ample faith. My intent was to help them better understand the love of God and grow in their own love for God and others.

After the message, Connie came up to me and said, "Pastor, I was raised in church and spent my whole life going to church and listening to sermons. You just preached the most powerful message on faith I have ever heard. You explained it perfectly and revealed my faulty faith. In fact, I realized today that I have not really trusted in Christ at all but have lived with doubt-filled disbelief, trying to convince myself I had faith. My eyes are open now. I now have faith in God, real faith, for the first time in my life. Thank you." As she walked away with tears of joy streaming down her face, I was puzzled, and the person I had been talking to when she approached was even more perplexed than I was. Listening to Connie's words, he said, "Whose sermon was she listening to? You did not talk about faith at all." I replied, "She was listening to God's sermon." I went on to explain that God reserves the right to communicate more fully through us, despite us, beyond us, and around us. God reserves the right to do more than we intend or expect. God reserves the right to shut our words out entirely and do his own sermonizing in someone's ears. He did it once (Acts 2), and he can do it again. God reserves the right to deliver people who we are not even aware that they need deliverance. God reserves the right to bring fullness to the situation—more than we think possible and more than we expect.

The Scriptures from Ephesians that I highlighted earlier in this chapter remind us that the fullness of God resides in Jesus Christ; the fullness of Jesus is found in the church and every believer. We refer to being filled with the Spirit. Different people have different thoughts in mind about the meaning of being filled with the Spirit. Without going into the differences churches have on how the Spirit fills and interacts with people, *filling* means that God has inserted himself into a person and the processes of their engagement. This fullness, as described in the Bible, lets us know that God is up to something higher, better, and more impactful than we could possibly understand.

Moses was preparing to deliver the people from Egypt to the Promised Land. Nine plagues down, with Pharaoh's heart getting harder and more resistant with each passing day. One more plague to go that would be the coup de grâce. God gave Moses specific instructions as to how that final plague would play out. Exodus 12 in its entirety is instructions and a description of the outcome for that evening. This included the most detailed explanation of a meal that would be known for centuries as the Passover.

The meal required eating a lamb without defect. Herbs and unleavened bread were part of the ritual meal. God instructed Moses to have the people use a hyssop branch to wipe blood on the top and sides of their door frames. There was no justification made for this and not much of an explanation as to *why* they were to do it. But there was detailed explanation of *what* would happen when they followed these instructions. God promised that the children of Israel would be spared while the children of

Egypt would die. God promised an escape after 430 years of oppression. He even forecasted that the Egyptians would give them more than the Israelites owned or requested with the hope they would leave and never come back.

There was a great deliverance that day. It should be remembered, however, that at the very beginning of God's instruction (Exodus 12:1-3), God was looking down the road at an annual celebration. A plan for the remembrance of this event was in place before the first Passover event took place. It was an additional layer of what God was planning that night. God was saving the people and planning to save many more in future generations. It was to be a memorial meal. But for what purpose? Was this just to be a reminder of God's deliverance from Egypt? Or was the meal also to serve as a promise of deliverance in the future? Two layers of meaning were set on one night: A life-changing event for the nation being saved, and a memorial for people to remember not only that God delivered, but that God delivers.

It was not until a Thursday night centuries later, when Jesus shared the Passover meal with his friends, that we get yet another layer of meaning to the story. It should not be wasted on the reader that the beginning of this night, from which flows an eternity of implications for all of us, has these as the first words, "Then came the day of Unleavened Bread on which the Passover lamb must be sacrificed" (Luke 22:7). The Bible does not say "Jesus wanted to have supper with his friends." This final layer to the deliverance story makes the Passover meal accessible for every person who would believe, demonstrating it is not just a meal commemorating the deliverance of a small nation of people more than a thousand years before. One event led to another and had huge implications for eternity. That is *pleroma*.

When Moses received the Passover instructions and passed them on to the people, there was no indication he thought that God had anything in mind beyond their immediate deliverance from Egypt. Moses conveyed instructions about how they would leave Egypt. He also let the people know that they needed to celebrate this day in memoriam for years to come. He likely thought there were two layers to this story. Case closed. But God had a grander plan in the works.

There are many examples of biblical stories that layer the here and now and the yet to come. Isaiah was a well-respected prophet, which was rare in his day. The nation of Judah had been threatened with destruction from a coalition of armies that included Israel and Aram. It did not look good for Judah. King Ahaz needed his faith bolstered, so God provided a sign. The sign was that even though the threat persisted, there would be a young woman (also could be translated as "virgin") who would give birth to a son and name him Immanuel (Isaiah 7:14). Before he would be old enough to discern right from wrong, the threat of the encroaching nations would disappear.

Sure enough, a baby was born under the terms described, and before the boy was old enough to know what was right or wrong, the threatening nations withdrew, and the people of Judah were at peace again, at least for a period of time. The boy's name was no doubt Immanuel. His prophetically descriptive name was Mahershalalhashbaz, which means "quick to the plunder, swift to the spoil." God did something needed in that day.

Anyone with at least a little understanding of the Scriptures would regard that as a good story and a name for the ages. Those of us who know more about the Bible understand that there is still another layer to that story. There was another woman, a real virgin, and there would be another child with the name Immanuel. There would be another understanding of the meaning of Immanuel (literally, "God with us"). There would be another deliverance. Next time, it would not be a deliverance from a couple of nations with bad intentions. It would be deliverance from a much more sinister foe—sin and evil. There was a second layer to this story that is so profound that most people have even forgotten the first story from Isaiah. Isaiah and his friends did not likely know there was anything more to that prophecy than what they experienced. Why would they? God promised them deliverance from two specific nations, and they received full deliverance. Case closed.

King David wrote Psalm 22, which communicates the prophetic nature of fullness as well. I am sure that David wrote this out of his own personal anguish. Anyone who has read his story knows he had ample anguish early in his life. Even though he later became king, he had his share of misery. He was betrayed by friends, attacked by a king he respected (Saul), was kept from developing his closest friendship (with Jonathan), he lost a son (Absalom), had a daughter raped by another son (Amnon), and had a host of attempts on his life while living in the wilderness and even in his own palace. He likely had no idea when he uttered his question to God—"My God, my God, why have you forsaken me?"—that it would be borrowed by one who truly was forsaken. His words were more powerfully spoken by Jesus from the cross. Jesus did not just feel forsaken but hung forsaken in every sense of the word. David spoke from his personal anguish.

Only in living long enough do we have the opportunity to understand the fuller meaning of our experiences. I have lived long enough to recognize several *pleroma* experiences in my own life. I have seen several fuller expressions or reasons for the experiences than I had years before.

Our family moved to the Philippines as missionaries where we served a three-year term. I was asked to be a missionary there for three primary reasons: to plant churches, to develop leaders, and to serve as the president of a Bible college. I did all three, and more. It was rewarding but a lot of work. We had left a thriving church—a wonderful congregation with good growth where I had developed many lifelong friends—to become missionaries. But in the Philippines, the romantic part of being a missionary quickly evaporated. I felt comfortable communicating in English for my entire life. I knew no other languages and had no desire to learn any. Then I had to learn and use Tagalog, and I was laughed at often for childlike errors in my speaking.

There is not enough room in this book to recount the humorous, embarrassing, and unintentionally insulting mistakes I made.

I had to learn a new culture that was markedly different from the American culture with which I was most familiar. Communication was different. Priorities were different. Effective leadership was different. Relationship development was different. Managing conflict was different. And some values and priorities were clearly different. I was rudely awakened to the fact that many things that I believed transcended culture were heavily influenced by culture. I learned with the gentle help of Ricky Serrano, David Clemente, Jim Tuan, Vicente and Isidra Prochina, Joyce Labrador, and others. Many times I was doing something I thought represented good leadership only to learn that I had offended someone not because of their immaturity but because of my cultural ignorance. Still, I learned how to pastor, lead, preside, and relate in that context. It became second nature. In fact, when we returned to the United States, I found myself a little less at home. I learned and even changed in some ways. I saw the world differently and responded to people differently.

With my primary work finished, we moved back to the United States, and the Lord made it clear to Marlene and me that he was leading us back to launch a church that would launch many churches and train leaders who would train many leaders. It was a bittersweet departure, and, I might add, a little confusing. After all our goodbyes and tears at the airport on our final day in the Philippines, our family of six settled into our respective seats on the jet, ready for our first trip home in three years. As we boarded the jet, I remember wondering why we moved to another continent and uprooted our children from their friends and family only to uproot them once again. Our children by that time called the Philippines "home."

Why would we learn a language and culture that we would not likely need in the future, devote ourselves to a ministry that we would not be able to see come to full maturity, and invest in so many relationships that would inevitably diminish over the years? Confusing, right? I remember pondering this with Marlene as we settled into our seats on the jet. At the end of the conversation, I asked the question, "What was that all about?" She said, "The Lord knows, though we don't."

Fast-forward twenty-five years later. We planted churches in the United States and developed leaders who have become pastors, missionaries, and educators. That was our hope and vision. That ultimately led to my election as a leader in the denomination in which we minister. In this new role, we return frequently to oversee ministry throughout Asia. The Lord has blessed the ministry and thousands of churches have been planted with wonderful, Spirit-filled leaders who possess vision, skill, and courage.

In one of those countries, Marlene and I were enjoying dinner with the national leaders, who were discussing in their own language the blessings of the Lord and the great growth they had experienced. Our translator was faithfully communicating every part of that conversation to us. Then, at one point, she stopped. I asked her why she stopped, and she simply asked me to wait for translation later. The conversation went on for about ten minutes without our involvement. To be cut out of the conversation seemed to be uncharacteristically rude for that culture. Finally, the group seemed to conclude its conversation. We ended with hugs, handshakes, and goodbyes. Then we departed.

In the taxi heading back to our hotel, I asked the translator in a frustrated tone, "Do you mind letting us know what was going on at the end of the meal and why you were not translating?" She said, "I'm sorry for leaving you out, but you were a big part of that conversation, and I wanted them to speak freely. They were saying how wonderful it has been to have an American leader who lived in a similar culture and understands their culture as a national leader would, leading and relating accordingly. They said they had not experienced that before, and it was a contributing factor leading to the ministry cooperation of all of the diverse groups here." Marlene looked at me and answered the question I asked on the jet twenty-five years earlier but had long forgotten. That's what that was about!

Pleroma is at work in those God is completing. It is impossible to know how everything fits together until it fits together. The prophets, kings, and apostles in the Bible did not know that they were part of something bigger. They did not know that their words and lives were leading to something beyond their immediate situation.

Project Me

- How can you "pay it forward" this week? Make a plan for it. If you can't think of an idea, talk to a trusted friend. Work together to make that first, small impact.

- Remember, *plemora* means "fullness." Think of a *plemora* experience in your own life. What is the fuller meaning that it has given to your life?

- Read Psalm 22. David wrote this psalm because of all he had suffered. Have you ever felt forsaken by a family member, a friend, or even God? After some prayer and reflection, write down all the ways God showed his faithfulness during this time.

3

Faith in God, Not in Resolution

I was on an international flight that had two long legs from the United States. The first was to Amsterdam, Netherlands. The connecting flight was to Mumbai, India. I often read, write, or try to sleep on long flights. Occasionally, movies are available at those times when I am too tired to do my usual routine. This was one of those occasions. I started watching a movie about eighty minutes before landing in Amsterdam, which wasn't a good idea. It was riveting—a captivating drama that unfolded with twists and turns. I could not at all guess where the plot would land. I was hooked. Then we landed. I waited impatiently for nearly four hours in the airport until I could board the next flight and resume the movie, which I did as soon as possible. I saw the ending and experienced the resolution I was looking for.

I have found that I do not like things to be unresolved. I want to hear the punch line of the joke or story. I want to finish a conversation. I want to get all the way to my destination without having to turn around, especially when I am driving. I want to finish the projects I start. I want to find out whether I made the team or not. I want to know if my team won or lost. I want to finish a meal I am enjoying without being whisked away in the middle of it, especially if I am still hungry. I want to hear the end of a song I am enjoying. I like seeing answers to my prayers. I want to see fruit from my faith and obedience. I want to see my children grow up. Whatever it is, I want to see or experience the results. And I have learned that I am not alone, because everyone appreciates resolution. Nearly every child who has been told it's time to leave when their parents were ready has said, "But it's not finished yet!" (in reference to whatever movie, game, or activity they're engrossed in).

Spoiler alert! We will not see the end until we are at the end ourselves. We will not find full resolution until all matters have been resolved. That is for certain. And yet, that is what most people want more than anything else. They want to experience the full resolution that cannot be experienced until the end. Don't get me wrong—this is not a matter of having peace or not. One can have peace while waiting. We can have that along the way. God provides peace even when the end is far away and turmoil surrounds us. I am not speaking of contentment. Like Paul, we can learn to be content regardless of our circumstance (Philippians 4:11).

However, many people, without knowing it, hold on to their faith in God only as long as they see God clearly coming through for them. In other words, their faith in God is less about God himself and more about his ability to produce. In those cases, faith often becomes more about resolution than God. Some people have faith in God only as far as they can see the possibility of resolution. For them, faith gives way to doubt, and they start wondering if God is really listening, really cares, or even exists if results are not forthcoming.

I know this is an issue since, as a pastor, I have seen it again and again and in multiple ways. Phil came to church as a desperate man looking for answers. Many people do. I talked to him after the worship service. He was visibly distraught. He looked like a man who had not slept in three days. He said his life was worth nothing since his wife decided to leave him for someone else. I listened to him and prayed for him, and we set an appointment to talk more deeply.

We met for lunch later that week. I asked him to consider shifting his primary goal to seeking God, trusting in him and allowing God to change him and make him into the person he was meant to be. I told him that God has the capacity to make him whole. Then, if his wife returned, a more whole and loving person would be there waiting for her to start a new chapter together. If she did not return, he could have a life that was not in ruins. I told him that if the starting and ending point was getting his wife back, then he may never discover what was broken in him and may never be able to trust and love completely without hesitation. He said he understood and would give it a go.

He prayed a prayer and said all the right things. But he could not get very far from revealing that his underlying faith was not in God; rather, he placed his faith in God's ability to answer one prayer the way he wanted—to bring his wife back. He came to Bible studies and prayer meetings. He met with a counselor and a men's group. He started being discipled by a man in the church who had similar experiences and in whom God had brought wholeness despite his wife never returning. Phil came to church and sang the songs. He listened to the sermons and said he was learning a lot from them. He got to know people and appreciated their care for him.

About three months went by, with Phil attending church weekly, before he asked for another lunch appointment. We sat together, and he poured out his heavy heart. He said, "I'm giving up on all of this. I don't believe in God anymore and can't trust anyone. God did not bring my wife back. I'm done!" That was only three months after saying, "I'm all in." His faith was in resolution rather than God. Or, if it was in God at all, it was contingent upon God's ability to produce the desired outcome. That did not work for Phil. It will not work for anyone. God wants us to believe in him, period.

I started my journey of faith in earnest when I was eighteen years old. The Bible was unfamiliar to me since I did not grow up in church, but I loved the Bible. I read it every day, a habit I have not stopped. Much of what I read made God and life seem clearer to me. Some things confused me a little. Some things just seemed odd altogether. Some of it inspired me greatly. One such inspirational passage was Hebrews 11. It spoke about people who had great faith. Many of them could be found in the pages of the Old Testament. I was able to dive deep into the details of their extraordinary faith by reading the Old Testament passages. I was moved by their faith and wanted faith like theirs.

On my third or fourth reading of that chapter, I stumbled onto a verse that I thought must be a mistake. It could not be correct. It simply did not ring true. Hebrews 11:13 says, "All these people were still living by faith when they died. They did not receive the things promised; they only saw them and welcomed them from a distance, admitting that they were foreigners and strangers on earth." I thought confidently, *That's not right!* God came through for all of them repeatedly. I could not come up with an explanation for verse 13. I thought that since there were only four people of faith mentioned prior to this verse (Abel, Enoch, Noah, and Abraham) that perhaps it was limited in some way to their unique experiences rather than making a broader statement about all the people mentioned in the chapter.

Then I came to verse 39, right near the end of the chapter, which implied the same thing about everyone in the chapter (Jacob, Gideon, Moses, David, Rahab, and several unnamed people): "These were all commended for their faith, yet none of them received what had been promised." Again, my initial thought was that these verses simply must be incorrect. It just did not seem right to say that these faithful people were clinging to their faith while still waiting for God to come through from a lifetime of unfulfilled promises. After all, they had received a bunch from God, including their own deliverance. This could not be correct. However, upon further inspection, I noticed that the things these people of faith had not experienced or received were the fulfillment of specific promises—the big life promises that we call covenants, or life promises upon which all other promises rest.

When we look at some of these, we see that in each case there was a big promise made by God. God made a specific covenant with them or a promise that impacted their whole future. In virtually every case, the people died without seeing it come to fruition. Abraham, Moses, and David are the clearest examples since we have more information about them and their interactions with God than the others.

Let's start with Abraham. God did many things for him. He called him and expanded his influence. God promised and gave him a lot of land and protected him when he was a stranger in that new land. He saved his son, Isaac, though Abraham was willing to offer him as a sacrifice. He gave him favor with the people around him. There was no doubt that God was with him. However, the big promise (covenant) that God entered into was never fully experienced by Abraham, even though God was clear and generous in telling Abraham what he would do for and through him. That big promise is in Genesis 12:2–3 when God said to Abraham, "I will make you into a great nation, and I will bless you; I will make your name great, and you will be a blessing. I will bless those who bless you, and whoever curses you I will curse; and all peoples on earth will be blessed through you." That was the promise (covenant) upon which all God's other promises rested.

God ultimately fulfilled his promise, as he characteristically does. Abraham never fully experienced the implications of it. His promise included becoming a great nation, and Abraham died without seeing a great nation rise up from his family. He had just one son of promise from which the nation would emerge, but he believed that God would give him a son as promised later in greater detail. Abraham continued to believe in God even though he never saw a nation come from his descendants.

God would bless all people on earth through Abraham. Abraham did not know all the people on the earth. He would not have known anything about South America or Africa or Europe. He surely did not know what the whole earth included. That promise could not have been fully understood, much less experienced, by Abraham in his lifetime. He continued to believe in God, not in resolution. And guess what? God resolved it even though Abraham never saw it.

Now let's turn to Moses, who is also mentioned in Hebrews 11. The covenant that God gave the people through Moses (Exodus 19–24) was based on a big promise that launched Moses back into Egypt to rescue the Israelites from slavery (Exodus 3). The covenant was for the people, and the promise related specifically to Moses and his role among the people. God spoke to Moses from within a burning bush (Exodus 3:4). The message was simple: God had a plan that included Moses extracting Israel from Egypt and leading the people to a "good and spacious land" (Exodus 3:7–10). All the other details in that chapter are subordinated to these elements. That was his whole calling: to get people out and safely into their new land. Moses was concerned about his role, so he argued with God about it. He wondered how he would execute the release of the Israelites. Moses predicted Pharaoh's resistance, but God was faithful and used him to deliver the people despite Pharaoh's threats. The deliverance was only the first half of the promise. The second half had to do with settling the people in the promised land.

Moses experienced the first part of the promise—the extraction. Sadly, he did not enjoy the privilege of settling the Israelites into the promised land, and he never crossed over the Jordan River in triumph, built a house in the promised land, planted a garden, or enjoyed its fruit. He was permitted to see it but not go there (Deuteronomy 34:1–5). Moses had a clear promise of what God would do, from deliverance to settlement. But Moses never saw the end of that promise. God did it as promised. Moses continued to believe God, though there was no resolution in his lifetime. Just like Abraham, his faith was not in resolution. It was in God.

David is another one of the faith-filled people of gigantic repute in Hebrews 11. David was king of Israel. He walked through unbelievable turmoil, and God was with him from the time of his anointing by the prophet Samuel (1 Samuel 16) until his last days as a king who died in peace during a peaceful time (1 Kings 2). After firmly establishing his kingdom, he turned his sights to how he might honor God. He came up with the idea of building a house (temple) for God. It was his idea, not God's. What came out of that desire was a revelation from the prophet Nathan, who said that David's descendants (and not David himself) would build a temple. We call 2 Samuel 7:8–16 "the Davidic Covenant." It contains God's response to David's request to build a temple.

God went one step further with David and said that he would not only allow David's son to build a temple but gave David the big promise that his kingdom would last forever. That promise went way beyond David's initial request. It is hard to imagine how David could even wrap his mind around the last part of this. After all, kingdoms rise and fall, and leadership lineages are broken up. That is a fact of history. How could God give him an endless kingdom and honor David's family like that? God went far beyond David's expectation and promised an endless kingdom under David's descendants.

Again, as with Moses and Abraham, this covenant to David contained two big promises that overshadowed all the others. This was the big ask and the big reveal. Though God had shown himself faithful to David throughout the years, the covenant God entered into with David near the end of his life would last forever. There were several components in it, including David's son Solomon building the temple and God building David's kingdom. It is worth noting that David would not see any of it.

The temple was not built before his death, and he did not see an endless kingdom either. He would be long gone before any part of the covenant was accomplished.

Solomon built the temple less than twenty years after David's death, and it was a whole millennium later that the angel Gabriel appeared to Mary with a promise that she would give birth to a son and name him Jesus: "The Lord God will give him the throne of his father David ... his kingdom will never end" (Luke 1:32–33). Gabriel heralded the promise given to David years before. Before long, the world eventually came to realize that Jesus established a kingdom that still has not ended. We can be confident in that.

Abraham, Moses, and David had faith in God whether or not they saw the full results of his promises. They knew that God was good for it. Their faith was in God, not in the resolution they knew he could provide. Their faith was that God would provide, not in the provision itself. It was great comfort for them to have God's promises, but their faith did not depend upon the promises. They received faith boosts along the way as God blessed them, honored them, and revealed himself to them from time to time. Nevertheless, make no mistake about it—their faith was in God and not contingent upon God giving them what they wanted.

That kind of faith is rarer in the world today than it should be. Many people do not live by faith alone but rely on visible, satisfactory results instead. We see it in the way that people plan their lives. Folks often make their plans based on expected outcomes rather than in obedience to God. The thought is this: *If it is not offensive to my morals or ethics, I would be crazy not to do what will produce the best results.* That kind of planning is based on how I believe things will work out (resolution) rather than how God wants me to obediently live.

I preached a message one day in a church I pastored. The church was packed with people, and we had multiple worship services. My time for visiting with congregants between services was minimal. I do not recall the subject of my sermon that day, but afterward I noticed it struck a chord with one woman, and she approached me. Nancy said with tears in her eyes, "Pastor, I have a dilemma, and I do not know what to do."

I asked her the obvious question, "What's your dilemma?"

She told me that Allyson, her roommate, business partner, and lifelong best friend, was having an affair with a married man. As her friend, Nancy didn't know what to do. She explained that throughout the sermon she believed strongly that God was telling her to lovingly approach Allyson and tell her of her concerns.

I asked again, "So, what is your dilemma?"

She looked a bit exasperated and said, "This is my best friend. I cannot lose this friendship. I would die if anything happened between us. She already knows I do not approve of that relationship and told me, 'If you try to dissuade me, then our friendship is over.'"

I asked once again, "So, what is your dilemma?"

She looked at me as though I was not listening at all.

I went on. "Nancy, as your pastor, I love you and want God's best for you, but you do not really have a dilemma as it relates to this situation. You are creating a dilemma. The only dilemma you have is knowing how to do what you know you must do. The problem is not whether or not you should say something to Allyson. You came to me saying that you know what God wants you to do. If you are convinced this is from the Lord, then you know what you must do, regardless of any difficult outcome that may result."

She said to me, "Okay! I will talk to my friend. But, if my relationship is ruined, I want you to know that you contributed to that."

I let her know that I have been charged with worse. She came to me for prayerful advice, and I gave it to her. I told her not to worry about outcomes. That is not our responsibility. Most things we worry about never come to pass.

Tuesday morning rolled around, and Nancy stopped by the

church on her way to work. She came into my office without stopping at the secretary's desk. "May I help you?" the secretary asked. She burst through the door and was grinning from ear to ear. She said, "I did it, and it worked."

I asked, "What worked?"

She told me how she called the married man's adult son. The son told Nancy that she should warn her friend about his father. He went on to explain that his father had done this kind of thing multiple times. He even volunteered to call Allyson and dissuade her, and he did just that. Between his conversation with Allyson and Nancy's loving pleading with her, Allyson was convicted and convinced. She called off the relationship with the man and humbly thanked Nancy for her determination and love. Smiling widely, Nancy said, "Our relationship has never been better. The past two days have been painful but wonderful." In the end, God brought about the resolution she desperately wanted anyway.

Nancy is not much different than all of us. We really want things to be resolved. We especially want the bad situations to be resolved with happy endings, just like the most endearing movies. We want to see the end and know that it will work out. If we cannot see it, how can we have confidence that it will happen? We have that confidence, not based on what we see but in whom we place our trust. If our confidence is in God and we know that he is loving and good, then such confidence should be enough. We have received many good things if we are in relationship with God. The beginning should give us confidence that, just as God has promised, so he will conclude the story well.

Project Me

- Think of a time when you sought solution that never came to fruition. Did you blame God? Did you give up like Phil? Think of a friend who is experiencing something similar. Give them a call, write them a note, or even meet up for coffee. Encourage them to not give up, and remind them that God is faithful!

- Did you ever face a major life decision, only to rely on your well-thought-out plan instead of God's leaning? Knowing what you know now, how might you alter your decision? And how has this influenced your current or future decision-making?

- Do you have a friend like Allyson who is turning down the wrong path? Is God convicting you to act on his prompting to help them? Prayerfully consider approaching your friend in love. Be confident that God will resolve the situation!

4

Walking in Light Rather Than Chasing It

Cats chase shiny things. They are good at it. A flashlight aimed at a wall will keep you and your cat entertained longer than you or the cat should want to be entertained. My family has had more cats than I care to admit. We have also spent more time exploring their fascination with light than I care to admit. I have tested the limits of my cats' leaping ability and sanity. In fact, there was a time when my flashlight received more use with cats than its intended purpose of aiding sight at night. (I was much younger then and spend my time more wisely now.)

I also love to fish—more than I have the opportunity to do so. Fish are not much different from cats. A shiny lure with a little sun reflecting on it can land a fish in the frying pan and result in a picture of the big one that did not get away. The sad thing for cats and fish is that chasing shiny things does not get them what they want or where they want or need to go.

Before we get too enamored with ourselves as living beings with higher cognitive skills than cats and fish, I could easily cite more examples of people chasing shiny things than any animal in creation, cats and fish included. Shiny objects have lured people for centuries. Modern marketing depends on this basic truth. The shinier the car and brighter the technology, the better. Whether literal light or figurative light, people chase light: movie stars, enlightened gurus, and flashes of success.

Marlene and I were returning home from Southern California on one of our many ministry trips. The line was long to get through security screening. We fly enough to land us on the TSA precheck list. Still, the security screening line was longer than usual that day. We had not been in line for more than three minutes before people started pulling out their cameras, aiming them in our direction and clicking away at an unbelievable rate. More people crowded around, getting nearer to us and continuing the flurry of picture taking. My initial thought was that these folks must be mistaking us for someone famous. Marlene, who is always more balanced than I am, had a more reasonable explanation: that someone around us must be famous. She was right; I was wrong. In front of us and behind us were the finalists for American Idol that year. They had just finished the competition and were heading home. Sadly, we were not knowledgeable fans at the time, so we did not know who they all were. We just squeezed in the line between some people with newfound fame. We were so close to being shiny ourselves that the attraction felt odd. After navigating through security, we returned to being our dull selves.

Don't get me wrong. I have taken my share of pictures of famous people and places even though I do not run after them. There is nothing inherently wrong with famous people. Many of them are humble servants of God. I have some friends who are famous. The deception about chasing shiny things is the thought that somehow we become more important when we possess something valuable or we are near someone who is considered more important than we are. It is a common error to think that chasing things that shine can make us more important or bring us satisfaction. It does not.

The lure of stardom, wealth, success, and power has led to the ruin of many. Chasing light was never God's plan for us. Light can be deceptively manufactured or imitated. Satan is good at creating cheap and destructive replicas of what God has created. The same is true with light. Satan himself masquerades as an angel of light (1 Corinthians 11:15). Chasing light is not a good idea. It can lead us where we do not want to go.

Walking in the light is something quite different. Walking in the light requires an existing experience and relationship. When we walk in light, we possess it rather than chase it. When a person walks in light, he or she is not looking at something alluring in the distance but living and moving in the moment with the Lord, who is light. John explained it well. He was the disciple who was arguably closest to Jesus in many ways. His brother was James. Both were fishermen when Jesus found them. He was in the security screening line (managed by the Pharisees, not the TSA) and standing next to Jesus for about three years. People were seeking to get close to Jesus, not purely because of his fame. They tried to get close to him for the help he could provide. John saw this daily and was caught in the press of the crowd on many occasions. He saw people come and go. John was walking with the light. Many of the needy seekers were chasing light. Most of them faded into anonymity and remain nameless. John, his brother, and a handful of others continued walking with Jesus, the light. They found love, grace, and truth in him. They walked with him and learned more about God and themselves than they ever could have walking on their own. John said:

> This is the message we have heard from him and declare to you: God is light; in him there is no darkness at all. If we claim to have fellowship with him yet walk in the darkness, we lie and do not live by the truth. But if we walk in the light, as he is in the light, we have fellowship with one another, and the

blood of Jesus, his Son, purifies us from all sin. (1 John 1:5–7)

He spelled it out. God is light. He is the real stuff. He is not masquerading. His light is not an illusion or a mirage. He is light. So, those coming to him, believing in him, and following him end up with what they might not expect—light. Those who walked with him were walking in the light, as John said. Put another way, when we run after God, we get light. When we chase after light, we never know what we will get. We will likely get more disappointment than light.

In 1 John 1:1–4, John talks about what he experienced in Jesus' presence—what he saw, heard, and touched—before reminding us that God is light. He experienced light and could not wait to tell others about it. In other words, he was walking in light and wanted others to join him. The difference between walking in light and chasing it is remarkable. People chasing light will look for what makes the most sense, gives the most momentary hope, and offers the greatest degree of personal satisfaction. Walking in light means that you already have the light and walk in hope and satisfaction. We do not need to chase anything. We need to simply walk with God, who is light, and allow him to make sense of everything in time.

God appeared to Abram (later Abraham) more than once—either in a dream, through angels, or in some other clear manner. That was light. Chasing the answer to those promises was unnecessary. Moses spoke to God directly in a bush and met with him, seeing his glory on a mountain for an extended period of time. That was enough. He did not need to enter the promised land. He had met the Promise Maker himself. Likewise, David never saw his kingdom prolonged. No need. He worshipped the King of kings and understood that the eternal establishment of God's kingdom was inevitable. He was content to walk in the light and play his part. He was not chasing long life or fame or wealth. He was content to walk in the light.

It was not just that they knew God was trustworthy and could be trusted. It was more than having faith in God instead of a resolution. They met God. They knew him. They worshipped him. They were walking with the God who is light and so they knew what to do next. They, along with the prophets, knew they had to act on what they knew about God and about what he wanted them to do. That is what John meant when he spoke about walking in the light. God is light. We stick with him regardless of what others say or what shiny things may be luring us in the distance. As long as our relationship with God is clear and clean, it's okay if our understanding of the future is a little unclear and muddy. After all, we know the end and have confidence that God can resolve everything. The book of Revelation is a puzzle, but we do not need to figure it out. We need to walk with the One who revealed it. If we know God, we know what matters. If we know God, we know everything will be okay in the end, and forever. We can live perfectly well not knowing how our days end here. If we know God for certain, we can live with the uncertainty about the specifics between now and our final days. That is walking in light rather than chasing it.

Not only did the prophets not know that there were layers to their prophetic utterances, but sometimes they were uncertain about the meaning of their prophecies altogether. They did not know how God would unfold things over and over. They were often clueless as to what their words meant in the near future, much less in the *pleroma* future. Daniel was a prophet who had some extraordinary visions about the future (see Daniel 7–8), but he did not know what they meant. In both chapters, he either sought or was given an interpretation by God (7:15–16; 8:15–16). He did not know what he was seeing or what it meant. The Lord obliged, but still, when he read the interpretations, they were muddy for him. The nations that were referenced in some cases did not exist when he was prophesying, and the symbols and numbers mentioned were never fully understood. How do I know? Because even with history in the rearview mirror, there are varying interpretations of his interpretations.

It was a high honor and privilege for Daniel to have God's trust. He became God's spokesperson for the kings of Babylon and Persia and the people of Israel in troubled times. Daniel loved God like no other and made it clear (Daniel 1), but his devotion to God irritated his jealous opponents and landed him in trouble (Daniel 6). Because of his walking in the light, he was entrusted with words from God and bestowed with occasional favor from the king. It did not matter if he fully understood the prophecies. He was simply doing what he did best—walking in the light of a relationship with God, serving God obediently and refusing to alter course because of a temptation or threat. We do not have a hint of Daniel ever chasing light, seeking fame, trying to understand the future, forecasting what might happen, profiting from his abilities, or adapting his messaging for the sake of appearances. People sometimes concoct visions or force interpretations in ways that increase their celebrity status. Daniel concocted nothing and did not labor to find interpretations. He was content to walk with God, to walk in the light. He sought neither notoriety nor wealth. He never chased light but walked in it and shared the light as it was given to him—no more and no less.

Daniel had some friends who were in the same boat at that time. Shadrach, Meshach, and Abednego were devout as well (Daniel 1; 3:12). They were walking in the light. They served God and depended upon him alone for protection. They had no connections that would protect them apart from God himself. They were not futurists, just as Daniel was not a futurist, even though the king thought he was. However, Daniel and his friends knew God well enough to know that being obedient to God would benefit them at times and land them in trouble at times. When faced with certain death, Shadrach, Meshach, and Abednego explained their faith to the king and his entourage. They essentially told the king that their faith in God had two components (Daniel 3:16–18): The first was their absolute confidence that God had the power to thwart the king's evil plans and protect them. The second was their admission that even if they were uncertain of the outcome, their faith would remain resolute. That is what walking in the light is like. It is to know God, remain confident in his ability, and serve him regardless of the outcome.

The list of prophets who similarly walked in light, eschewing the temptation to chase it, is impressive: Moses, Elisha, Jeremiah, Jonah, Obadiah, Elijah, Micaiah, Nathan, Amos, and a host of nameless prophets. They all found themselves in trouble with earthly authorities for their words. In some cases, they were reluctant to prophesy at all. Moses, Jeremiah, and Jonah went so far as to argue with God about how he was using them. They were not at all interested in seeking the limelight. (Jonah could not have been more obvious in his flight from notoriety.) None of them were interested in gaining fame because of their prophecies.

Centuries later, Jesus let it be known that Jerusalem and its leaders represented by that city's distinct name were infamously killing God's prophets (Luke 13:34–35). It is not as though Jesus was the only one in history who knew his fate if he spoke for God. The prophets knew it did not bode well for them if they spoke the truth. Jeremiah knew he would be in trouble if he spoke for God. He certainly would have preferred someone else to be bestowed with the dubious honor of prophesying terrible things to people that did not want to hear it. Still, he was the one chosen for the task, and he did it out of obedience to God. At the same time, he did not hesitate to complain about it (Jeremiah 20:7–18). Eventually, he did it. He was not chasing fame or acceptance. He was just walking in the light.

When Jesus spoke about the murder of prophets, he implied that he was next (Luke 13:31–33). And, like the other prophets, he was not chasing light at all. He was not running away from his death. Nor was he running to gain fame. He was doing the will of his Father (John 6:38). His focus was walking in light, not chasing it. In fact, he called himself the Light of the World (John 8:12; 9:5) and encouraged people to walk in his light. He called others to relationship with him just as he had a relationship with the Father.

In modern terms, we have a unique way of differentiating between chasing light and walking in light. I hear many people talking about following your dreams. That is a chasing light statement. It is remarkably different than following Jesus Christ, which is a walking in light statement. Following dreams means that we have an ideal, and everything impeding or getting in the way of it is seen as an obstacle. Those experiences are distractions to reaching our goal. I have heard people say, "Don't let anything stop you from reaching your dreams." However, what if our dream is not God's ideal? What if the distraction is not a distraction at all, but misdirection? What if the thing we consider an impediment is the Spirit telling us there is something more important?

The person who walks in light is following Jesus Christ, not a dream. They are following a person, not a possibility. They are following God's desire, not their own. We may just find that the unwelcomed experience is a teachable moment, a needed correction, or an exercise in obedience.

Jesus implied this strongly in a parable he told a religious leader who was both an expert and a professional on religious matters (Luke 10:25–37). The question posed by the religious leaders about inheriting eternal life was most likely disingenuous, and his follow-up question about interpreting the Law was intended to lead Jesus into a maze of definitions. We also leave the story without a word about his reply or desire to change. His question to Jesus was what he had to do to inherit eternal life. He plied Jesus with Jesus' own words, and Jesus answered him by quoting the Shema (what we call the Great Commandment). Every religious leader knew the Shema to be the pinnacle of purpose. No argument there. Love the Lord God with heart, mind, soul, and strength. Everyone knew the right answer. Jesus went a bit further and quoted another passage from the Old Testament, adding to also love your neighbor as yourself. That received no pushback either. Then, the religious leader revealed his intent to be less than noble by asking a distracting follow-up question about who his neighbor was.

Jesus could always tell the difference between people searching for truth, seeking help, looking for an argument, or trying to pick a fight. He recognized the religious leader's faulty motive though we may have been fooled. Jesus often used a parable to speak directly to the situation and the motive of the person asking the question. This encounter was no exception.

Most people reading this story (the Good Samaritan) look at the obvious point Jesus was making. The religiously astute leader needed to be taught a lesson about what it means to love God and love people. What better way to teach it than to show that religious individuals can easily be outshined in the love department by a despised Samaritan? The priest and the Levite in Jesus' story passed right by a man in desperate need. The Samaritan, who was not constrained to follow the Jewish law, demonstrated compassion on the man who had been robbed and beaten. He knew intuitively and practiced what the religious people studied but did not practice. *Touché!*

However, there are often layers of meaning in Jesus' stories and teachings. There are certainly some other implied truths Jesus was making, like the complete redefinition of neighbor. Jesus forever changed the definition of neighbor in this parable from someone nearby to the person who needs me the most. Our neighbor is anyone we can help, not just someone whom society says deserves our help based on proximity and importance.

Another meaning here exposes the difference between people chasing light or walking in it. All three people (the priest, Levite, and Samaritan) were walking between Jericho and Jerusalem and had someplace to go. The man who was robbed likely had things to do as well, but his journey was tragically interrupted. The three people who came upon the man whose religion, race, and devotion are not exposed are irrelevant to the need for compassion. They had two options—keep moving or stop and help. One exercised compassion and chose to walk in the light. Two did not.

We must be reminded that all three leaders on the road that day likely loved someone and something. At the end of the parable, Jesus did not ask, "Who had love?" Rather, he asked, "Which of these three do you think was a neighbor to the man who fell into the hand of robbers?" (Luke 10:36). Jesus noted at other times in his preaching that a person can love one thing or another, such as God or money. But, if they are at odds, it is difficult to love both. Whether that love is more noble or less noble does not eliminate the possibility of loving different things (Luke 16:13; John 21:15). In the same way, our priorities and focus will always align with our love. In this case, giving the option of valuing the destination or the hurting man, two of the sojourners chose the destination over the man. They chose safety, order, and convenience over the disruption caused by the mess of dealing with messes.

The two passing on the other side of the road placed their destination as more important than ensuring the wounded man received medical attention. It may have been the physical destination where they were heading, or it may have been the figurative destination where they were heading (reputation, esteem, or success). Either way, where they were going was more important than where they were. What they had to do in the future was more important than what they should do in the present. The people they were going to see at their destination were more important than the man lying in desperation. That is the difference between walking in light and chasing it. People chasing their priority will always seek their destination first, but people walking in their priorities will always see what is most important along the way.

For those who chase light, obedience is a means to an end. For those who walk in the light, obedience is the end. We should never act obediently in order to get where we would like to go. We do not act out of obedience because it will get us the results we want. That is chasing light and using our obedience as a means to get there. Walking in light means that we simply want to do what is right in any given moment. We want to love as God taught us to love. Remember, love is not something we plan. We love only because love is in us. We act obediently because we are walking close to God and want to please him, serve him, and live the calling he gave us.

That is precisely what the Samaritan did. He had places to go just as the others did. He apparently had money as well since he was able to not only get the victim what he needed but promised to do more upon his return. It was not as though the Levite and priest were important and busy but the Samaritan was not. He had means and was well-traveled. Acting out of love, which was Jesus' original reminder to the expert in the law listening to the parable, the Samaritan subordinated his long-term goals to do what only loving people can do—sacrifice their interests for the interests of God and others.

I live in a land with many resources. According to every measurable statistic, Americans have more wealth than most of the world's populations. We have the capacity to plan, store up, prepare, and execute long-range goals. We predict trends, build alliances, and partner more broadly because of the resources, technology, and access we have at our disposal. In other words, we can prepare to do good in hundreds of ways, but all the planning and resources available to us does not mean that we will always use them to meet the need of the neighbor instead of for reaching the goals we have set.

I have had the benefit of traveling the globe. Marlene and I have lived in three countries and visited over sixty. We have noticed that in many places where there is less infrastructure and fewer resources, the people are sometimes more responsive to the needs around them in the moment. Not always, but often this is the case. We have seen people carry sick and injured loved ones for days to a place where they can get help. Of course, I am neither saying that Americans are heartless nor that all people in less developed countries are generous. Some of the most generous people I know live near me and have lived sacrificial lives, benefitting thousands through their generosity. I have similarly seen my share of thieves and scoundrels elsewhere. What I am saying is that in places where we can think down the road and have the resources to chase dreams, we often do. We can eliminate the temptation of distractions, but what if those distractions happen to not be distractions at all but attempts to remind us what it means to be human and opportunities to live in obedience and express love?

It is interesting to note that Jesus performed many of his miracles while he was on the way to somewhere else. He healed a woman on a crowded road while en route to raise a girl from the dead (Mark 5:21–43). He healed a couple of blind men as he was leaving Jericho on his way to his most important and final destination, Jerusalem (Matthew 20:29–34). On the way to Jerusalem, Jesus encountered many people who sought his help. At one stop, ten lepers, who were socially prevented from approaching Jesus, shouted at him from a distance, begging for help (Luke 11:17–19). He stopped and told them to show themselves to the priest. As they went, they were healed. Again, Jesus was going somewhere. He was not loitering or sight-seeing. His goal was out there—his big goal. But that goal did not prevent him from loving those who needed love along the way. Why? He was walking in light, not chasing it. He lived in love in the present with an eye to the future.

One day I was running late to my appointment to teach the Good News to people in a very poor area of Letre in Malabon, Philippines. I had planted a church there. That was the first church in that area that was not a Catholic church. It was in a slum where most of the people lived in makeshift huts. In that area of Letre, many were homeless altogether, without even a kubo (hut) for cover.

Since I was running late that day, I was trying to prepare my message along the way. I took a bus so I could read and write. My Tagalog was still rough, and I needed to memorize the Bible verses I was using in that language. I was reading and writing as quickly as I could. I had a goal.

I stepped off the bus and walked down a poor excuse for a road, reading my Bible while walking. My peripheral vision was enough to keep me from stepping on a board with a nail or a sick, sleeping cat. I was focused on the Bible and my goal of teaching. My vision was physically and spiritually ahead of me. On my way, I stepped over a lifeless body without being distracted from getting to my destination. I was just about finished memorizing my text for the day, "Come to me all you who are weary and burdened and I will give you rest" (Matthew 11:28). About twenty steps farther, it dawned on me that the person I had stepped over was either dead or dying. I turned around, went back, and knelt by him. His lips were barely moving. I had some water and wet them. He was not very responsive. I sat with him until he died, moved him to a place where he would be out of the way, and sent some of the locals to see if he had any family. He did not. He was a homeless man who had been there for more than a day without moving.

We delayed our service for a couple of hours. I do not even remember what happened in the worship service. But I remember our brief service for him the next day. Stepping over a dying man to get to my goal without flinching or noticing him is one of my greatest regrets in life. Going back to do what I should have done in the first place is one of my most humble corrections. I was chasing truth and love when I should have been attentive and walking in it. Walking in the light is what we were called to do. The apostle John's coaching on this point is of utmost importance in our quest to complete "project me."

Project Me

- Have you ever encountered a celebrity and been awe-struck? What character traits does your favorite celebrity have that makes them attractive?

- What is the difference between chasing the light and walking in the light?

- As you attend to your various tasks this week, be intentional and stop for someone that you might normally pass by without a second thought. Buy them a coffee, ask them how they are doing, etc.

PART I SUMMARY

God finishes what he starts. What he has not yet finished, he will. The record is clear. Among the many works he promised to start and finish are the people he created who believe in him (Philippians 1:6). We need to believe him and trust him to make sense of our lives and finish the project we want completed more than anything else—the project that is our own lives. We want our lives to be fulfilling, purposeful, and significant, as well as eternal. He wants that for us even more than we do. Our role is to believe, respond, and obey.

God is up to much more than anyone knows. Just consider the stories of the prophets, kings, priests, and apostles. Virtually everything that happens in life has the potential to be more than anyone thinks possible. Each event in our lives, whether we see the impact in the present or not, has the potential to be used by the Lord, whether it's extremely painful or seems completely insignificant. Occurrences that seem to be nothing but trouble for us have potential for good. God uses our life experiences to influence our growth and the growth of others when we least expect it. He will reveal it in time. We must believe that he "is able to do immeasurably more than all we ask or imagine" (Ephesians 3:20). We must live with anticipation, trusting that more is coming from each experience. Look for it. Expect it. Just do not hurry it. By hurrying results, we hurry God.

God wants us to place our faith in him rather than our hopes. Hopes are necessary, but they just make bad objects of our faith. The irony is that the more we trust in God, the more hope we have and the more our hopes are realized. If we place our faith in God only for what he will produce, the less we'll see produced. Our relationship with God becomes tainted when we make it conditional. If we place our faith in God, knowing that he will do what is right regardless of our expectations, we have confidence and can rest in his ability rather than our desires: "The one who calls you is faithful, and he will do it" (1 Thessalonians 5:24). He is faithful and the greatest power we can exercise is faith in God.

God gives us ample light to walk in, not to chase. Every person has the opportunity to do what is most needful, to love and obey. The ancients in the Bible found that walking with God was much more effective than chasing light. We must not become preoccupied with what might be. We must be deeply committed to doing what God wants us to do now: "Seek first his kingdom and his righteousness, and all these things will be given to you as well" (Matthew 6:33). There is no need to seek for what might be. Seek God and find the things that he has prepared.

Sovereignty is a descriptor of God's dominance and impact in the world. Fullness (*pleroma*) is a descriptor of how his sovereignty works in the events and experiences of our lives. He does more than we will ever know. We must not look at each event as a one-off occurrence. God will continue to unpack purpose and meaning throughout our lives. Look at your life as a tapestry, not a snapshot. God is still weaving the results.

In part 2, we turn our attention to what this looks like today. You may see your life as a mundane existence; a life that has seemingly disconnected twists and turns, a fun ride without much rhyme or reason, a purpose-filled life that is well ordered, or one that is good but has been disrupted by unforeseen tragedy. However you view your life, *pleroma* is at work. We will explore how.

PART 2

What Fullness Looks Like Today

5

Ripples, Threads, and Endless Impact

When I was about ten years old, my father took our trailer to Beaver Lake where he was working on a job. It was summertime. He invited me to accompany him. While he worked vigorously, I spent most of the time hiking, fishing, and swimming in the lake. One morning the lake's surface was like glass. There was not a whiff of wind. The mountains and sky on the other side of the lake reflected perfectly in mirror image. If gravity hadn't betrayed which way was up, it would have been difficult to tell which scene was real and which was the reflection.

I was an active and precocious child. I simply could not allow that lake to remain so still. I yielded to the temptation to disrupt the order, picked up a rock, and hurled it as far as I could out into the lake. It made the intended splash, and I learned something about physics. All I wanted and expected to do was make a quick splash and walk away knowing that the reflection was disrupted, but as I stood there and watched the water, I saw the whole lake transform. I could not just walk away. The ripples from the rock I threw disrupted the entire lake, which was more than a half-mile long and quarter-mile wide. The ripples just kept going. The reflection was diminished. The stillness was interrupted. I stood and watched for what seemed like ten or fifteen minutes until, as far as I could see, the ripples impacted the entire lake from shore to shore.

The ripples were like an echo only they were longer lasting and more pronounced. With echoes, we intend to make one sound with two, three, or four sounds answering back. Those ripples on that day did not stop until the shore drew the line after minutes of motion. Unlike an echo, the ripples seemed to continue in perpetual motion until yielding to a hard edge.

Newton's third law of motion postulates that for every action there is an equal and opposite reaction. And I suppose it is true when it comes to the laws of motion. But what I experienced at the lake did not seem to represent that law fully. Sure, I threw a big rock, and it made a big splash. But I thought the splash was a satisfying enough opposite reaction. The ripples seemed to emerge from nowhere and just kept going. It took one second for the rock to collide with the water and make the intended splash, but the subtle reverberations continued across the surface of the lake for a long time.

It was not until years later that I drew a parallel: After the big splash, more will follow. When God speaks or acts, we see and hear action. We expect an equal and opposite reaction. Sometimes it is bigger than expected or the consequences are bigger and longer than we can comprehend. In those cases, the implications go on for centuries. God can do one thing for one generation, and it can affect generations to come. Likewise, we do things more often than we know that can have consequences for years to come.

The laws of motion do not apply to the laws of God's working or God's morality. We may want them to. We may hope they do. We may live as though they do. But they do not. God created the world in short order. The breathing response of creation has reverberated for millennia. The first man and woman sinned, and we are still assuming the guilt and carrying on the same kind of sordid behavior. We are still living under the same sentence of death. One man stole, hid, and lied, and the whole nation paid the consequences (Joshua 7–8). One woman took a single risk and saved a nation from extermination (Esther 7–9). Another man died, and the whole of humanity now has access to benefit from his death (Romans 5:17–19). In each case, the consequences of both sin and righteousness went far beyond what was anticipated by those observing. Even most of the people in these examples from Scripture were oblivious to the long-term impact of their actions.

The laws of God and his laws of morality are different than the laws of motion. People want them to be the same. I know it. In fact, sometimes I want it. When a person steals something, they generally think of the immediate benefit of the theft. They do not anticipate the unexpected pain they've undoubtedly caused the person they stole from, the prospect of legal action being taken against them, the shame and disapproval of family members when they learn of the theft, and the guilt that remains whether recognized or not, or the loss of innocence and the propensity to repeat an unpunished offense. The notion that there is one equal and opposite reaction to our sin is foolishly mistaken. The ripples continue.

The same is true for acts of righteousness, confession, valor, and courage. How often have we heard someone say, "I just did it because it was the right thing to do," or, "I did not realize that it would inspire so many people." They are surprised by the spreading joy or numbers of people who have benefitted from their action. They were just doing what was right. In their cases, maybe they were not expecting an equal and opposite reaction, or any reaction at all. If they were expecting a response, they likely got more. Medal of Honor recipients, organ donors who did what they felt was necessary, people who have given sacrificially to help marginalized people, and friends who helped someone overcome addiction generally hoped for one outcome—the saving of a life. Often, they not only saved a life but inspired others. They often helped the person who was saved continue to achieve great things in life and in turn help countless other less suspecting beneficiaries from their actions. People of character generally think more about what is right than creating ripples of righteousness.

Like the ripples on Beaver Lake, the consequences of an action reverberate much longer than the initial "splash." In fact, the impact of the splash itself affects two or three feet of the lake, depending upon the size of the rock. The ripples, on the other hand, affect the entire lake. The duration is longer than the splash, and the scope is greater than the splash. Actions are like that. So are words. How often does someone say something good or hurtful, expecting a single response, only to discover that their words have blessed or hurt beyond measure? It happens all the time. Many have said after a rash outburst, "I wish I could take those words back. I had no idea those words would hurt so many, damage my reputation, and break trust with so many people. It was one moment that has dogged me for years."

I have also watched a brief word of hope sustain a person for years or encourage a nation to persevere through trials. A single speech has inspired a nation to dramatic change. Martin Luther King's "I Have a Dream" sermon sparked a sustained revolution of human rights. Patrick Henry's speech to the Second Virginia Convention was a tipping point for Americans to prepare for their fight for independence. Nelson Mandela's "I am Prepared to Die" speech is hailed as the most compelling speech leading to the end of apartheid in South Africa. Abraham Lincoln's brief speech in Gettysburg (only 272 words long) both honored the dead and inspired a nation to complete a course that would ultimately heal a seemingly unhealable conflict. Words that still have ripples of influence in the world today.

God spoke, and the world came into existence. The ripples of his words, "Let there be …," continue to this day. Jesus' final words to his disciples, before he ascended to heaven, could not be completed by them alone, and he knew it. Jesus said, "But you will receive power when the Holy Spirit comes on you; and you will be my witnesses in Jerusalem, Judea, Samaria and to the ends of the earth" (Acts 1:8). He was telling them to make the splash and let the ripples continue. And, in a way, this is what has been happening over the past 2,100 years. I am one of millions of ripples that have resulted from the splash of the apostles' testimony. These ripples last for eternity.

Let me use another analogy—threads. That said, I am not a tailor. I do not understand how garments are constructed. Years ago, I tried to mend some pants that were torn. In my attempt to redeem the pants, I ruined them to the point that they were no longer good for anything but oil rags. It makes little sense to me how just one of many independent threads can impact a whole garment. I have been reminded many times about the connection between threads.

A while ago, Marlene and I went to a Broadway show. We wore semiformal clothes to the event. But first, there was dinner. During dinner, I noticed one thread protruding ever so slightly from my slacks. It formed a bulging loop. It made sense to pull that loop out or cut it off with scissors to restore the perfect look. I tried pulling it, thinking, *What could go wrong?* Surely an expensive pair of slacks would withstand a little thread pull. Instead, I ruined my pants, and we made our way quickly to a fine clothing store to buy new pair for the evening. Threads might be small, but together they form an intricate fabric. Each separate strand impacts the texture, color, line, and shape of the fabric, and their individual importance should not be underestimated.

While we were teaching in Nepal many years ago, we had the opportunity to tour a factory where decorative tapestries, rugs, and carpets were made. Our host told us that this factory was famous for the carpets and wall hangings it created. Their tapestries were hung in palaces and kingly estates, and some of their rugs were centerpieces on the floors in famous banquet halls and sitting rooms. Many of their tapestries sold for tens of thousands of dollars. We ended up buying two small throw rugs.

They were worth a few hundred dollars rather than a few thousand. We simply had to get them after we saw the painstaking operation.

It was hard to believe that anything beautiful could come from the factory floor. The looms and machines were not new. In fact, they could have been centuries old for all I knew. The loom shafts were worn. The warp beams were shiny from wear. It was hard to discern whether the heddles were wire or cord. The shuttles took on shapes of their own after years of being thrown back and forth, rubbing on the thread. They seemed to develop shape like the fingerprints of those who used them. The building itself was a drab factory. The only color in the room were in the small threads which were soaked in large vats with roots, flowers, and other plants that had been ground into powder and liquefied.

The Nepali and Tibetan women made the finished tapestries and rugs from drawings. There were no instructions. They were focused on the thread and the machine. It was masterful! They promised us that our rugs would look as good after ten years of walking on them as they did that day. They were right. We have been walking on them for more than a decade, and they still have the same beauty as the day we brought them home.

The threads did not seem to be connected at all when they remained in the vats or on big spools. There was nothing artistic about the individual threads when they were in rows on the warp and the weft. The artistic nature of the rugs could not be seen by the naked eye. It wasn't until all the threads were connected in tight harmony that one could see the beauty. Threads—do not take any of them for granted. No matter how unassuming, they can be part of an amazing finished product.

That is how life works. In this way, life is more like art than science. There are pieces, thousands of them. The pieces look like experiences, relationships, and events. Many of them are good. Many of them are bad. Many of them are expected. Many are complete surprises. As stand-alone elements, they seem to make life interesting but not necessarily more understandable. The pieces all have color and texture, yet they look like disconnected, drab strands of fabric. It is hard to believe that they could possibly be put together as a whole, but they can. In fact, they must.

God takes it all. He is working on this project that he started, and he will use it all. When the threads are put together, the artistry of what God can do takes shape. Colors emerge that did not exist in isolation. Texture unfolds to give depth and meaning to life as it is lived out. God uses everything if we patiently allow him and willingly participate with enough interest and curiosity to at least see what he is up to.

We may not be the first ones to know the impact of our varied experiences, and we may not be the first ones to recognize their connections. I think we are often the last ones to know who is being impacted and how they are impacted. It is often those who stand at a distance who see the beauty or the meaning of our experiences. Standing close to a tapestry does not necessarily give you the same impression as standing at a distance. It is only when the product is nearing completion that we can see how it has all worked together.

One of the greatest men I have had the privilege of knowing is Jake DeShazer. You can read about his interesting life story in his book *Love Your Enemies, From Bombs to Bible* or any number of books or movies about his life. Jake was one of Doolittle's Raiders, a bomb squadron who flew a retaliatory strike over Japan in the early years of World War II, shortly after the Japanese bombed Pearl Harbor. He was the bombardier of a B-25 that successfully carried out a bombing raid over Nagoya, Japan. However, Jake's plane ran out of fuel, and he, along with others, ended up being the longest-held American prisoners of war in World War II. He was one of the few survivors of their forty months of imprisonment, and Jake spent thirty-four months in solitary confinement. Three of Jake's squadron were executed by firing squad. Another died of slow starvation. Jake was near starvation at times and beaten frequently during his years in the prison camp.

Jake convinced one of his captors to smuggle a Bible to him. He became a Christian in prison camp. His life and character changed. Having become proficient in Japanese, he was able to communicate with his captors, as they were his only human contact. He started treating his abusers with respect and found himself investing in their lives with loving concern. Ultimately, after his release from imprisonment at the end of the war, he went to college in preparation to become a missionary and head back to Japan. His story contributed significantly to Mitsuo Fuchida's conversion to Christianity. Fuchida, ironically, was the Japanese commander who led the attack on Pearl Harbor. Jake learned Japanese and the love of God while he was in prison. Jake later returned to Japan to become a missionary where he served for over thirty years. He and Fuchida became the most unsuspecting and mutually respecting friends. They were like brothers in the Lord working together.

I spoke with Jake on many occasions. He recounted how his Christian upbringing was somewhat uneventful and seemingly unimpactful. Jake did not consider himself to be a person of profound faith. He came to know some Scripture through the more traditional Sunday school memorization activities. But, as he grew, he did not always live them out and thought he had forgotten most, if not all, of them. Jake had good relationships with family and friends, and he learned to be loyal to those people he knew and cared about. He did not consider himself to be deeply effusive in his expressions of love, but he knew how to listen and learn from others. Jake learned the value of hard work and understood how to live out a commitment. If he would ever need resolve, he had developed a habit of resolve, patience, and endurance. He was particularly adept at relating with challenging people. Because of some challenging relationships, Jake had ample opportunity to live that out in his early life. He understood how to bring calm and repair to that which was broken.

Then, when Jake found himself in a prison camp, the threads were all woven together. He was changed by God's grace. The whole world around him changed. God started putting the threads together to make a beautiful tapestry. Later, Jake admitted to me that he just did not see it until others saw it. He impacted many others in ways that brought about change in their lives. The end product was the development of one of the most kind, considerate, and loving people I have ever known. He has long passed on, but the gentle and sweet man he was conjures memories with his family and friends of a generous lover of God and people. The finished tapestry was one of the most beautiful life tapestries I have ever seen.

It never ceases to amaze me how human nature leads us to look at the events of our lives and our relationships as a bunch of disconnected threads. If there is color, it has no artistic definition. Most often, the events of our lives are viewed as one-offs. Most relationships are viewed as disconnected. After all, there does not seem to be any rhyme or reason to who we know and why we know them. There often seems to be no larger connection in these relationships other than our random knowledge or people. Our random experiences seem to be just that—random. Some are good and some are bad. Some lift us up, and some tear us down. The skills we have developed fit our vocations at times, and sometimes they seem to have little bearing on how we work or live our lives. But the ripples they cause in our lives have symmetry. The threads eventually start to connect.

Like ripples on a lake, the impact of the events of our lives extends farther than we could imagine. Like threads, all the pieces, people, and places start making sense if we have eyes to see them. There is more to your life than what you can possibly see from where you are standing now. In fact, there is more to your life than you will ever know in this life. The ripples will outlive your body, and the thread of your life will be woven into the threads of other lives in unsuspecting and sometimes invisible ways.

I know many interesting people. I have met or become friends with country leaders, inventors, drug addicts, famous musicians, infamous criminals, notable authors, and inconspicuous laborers. Each of them has had an indelible impact upon others. Each of them has had opportunities, challenges, and unique connections that no one else has had. Many of them have had an indelible impact upon me. The impact of some has been inestimably good and at other times it has been painfully tragic. They all have stories comprised of decisions, actions, relationships, experiences, and events that surpass their intentions.

The most interesting people I know do not fully understand how they arrived where they are today. They would admit that they ended up in places that they never expected. It is only after years of reflection that a person can start to see the developing shape of their lives. The most interesting people I know have had many varied and unconnected experiences, lived in unusual combinations of places, and have known diverse kinds of people. That is partly what makes them so interesting. They have a soup of experiences, relationships, and skills. Indeed, it is a tasty soup with all those ingredients.

In each case, the impact of their lives is endless. The ripples continue to roll. Each event, relationship, experience, and decision reverberates well beyond its initial splash. There are so many interconnected threads, with each one dependent upon the other. It is impossible to see where it all ends. I have been changed by hearing the story of people who passed away long ago, people I never met. Their impact continues. I have read life-changing words from authors who have been in the grave for more than three hundred years. I have been changed by the death and resurrection of a man who was laid in a grave more than two thousand years ago. The ripples stop at the shore. But what if the shore is eternity and not the grave? If that is the case, we will never see the end. If our grave is not the end, then it must be something else.

If God is starting a good work in us, then he is the designer. We have opportunity to respond to his good work, and we respond our whole lives, whether we know it or not. Some respond well, others poorly. The result of our lives are consequences—a lot of consequences—both good and bad. The ripples roll, and the threads connect. Every piece of your life matters, and it is never beyond God's ability to redeem, restore, and use our lives. Never forget that. When yielded to God, your life can be an instrument of great worth and impact. Just do not walk away so quickly when you think the impact is over. I started walking away from Beaver Lake after the big splash. I do not know what made me turn around and take a second look. I am forever glad that I did. My little arm did more than I realized had I just thrown the rock and walked away.

Turn around and take a hard look at the ripples. Contemplate how God is weaving the threads together to complete you.

Project Me

- Think of a time you did something (good or bad) that had an impact for several days (or even weeks or months) afterward. What were the immediate and long-term results of your actions?

- Who in your life has passed on but left a beautiful tapestry of their life behind? What were some of their most admirable qualities?

- Spend time in prayer today talking with God about the impact that you would like to leave. What kind of ripple will you leave behind?

6

Time + Faith + Obedience = Answers

Time is about as measurable and constant as anything in the world. It is like gravity. Nothing else is quite as predictable and stable. We can make appointments three years in advance and get a reminder fifteen minutes before the event. We can jump on the phone the same time as someone else halfway around the world with no gap or misunderstanding. Google helps with that. But it can only help because they are able to program it in. Time is programmable. Or at least objective time is programmable.

We even use expressions such as "It went like clockwork," or "You could set a clock by that," indicating how predictable something or someone is. Time has no give or flexibility to it. We all get twenty-four hours in a day.

There are few things that are as inconsistent or irregular as subjective time. There is nothing more flexible than time when it comes to our response to it. Subjective time is quite different than objective time. It is either interminably long or flies by so quickly that we have trouble believing the clock and calendar. For a child waiting for the last day of school to end before summer break, time is interminably long. For the soldier awaiting deployment at the base, those last few moments seem as though they are moving too quickly. For the person waiting for the results of a biopsy, the clock seems to pause. For the elderly, it's as though it was just yesterday that their children were young and in school. Time flies by when a person is engaged in something that envelopes their attention. Have you ever been engrossed in a good book, movie, or conversation and time slipped by so quickly that it made you late for an appointment? I have.

Subjective time is measured not by what time is but by how it feels. It is not about the actual science of time but how it affects us. And therein lies the problem. Time affects us. For those who want something to happen that is not happening, there is something wrong with the clock or God or the whole world. It does not seem to be working in their favor. For the person who does not want something to end, they feel as though the clock or God or the whole world is pushing them too quickly. We tend to look at time as either our friend or our enemy. (Most often it's perceived as our enemy.) In all of this, God is often the scapegoat or culprit when, in reality, he is not impacted by our sense of immediacy or desire to stretch experiences out. That is not God's primary concern. Our completion and development is.

I have often wondered how God perceives our fickleness when it comes to time. We are capricious at best. For him, time serves a different purpose. God seems to be more concerned about the completion of things rather than the immediacy or the suspension of them. Perhaps that is why the Bible tells us to pray without ceasing (1 Thessalonians 5:17). We should always be in a spirit of prayer since God does not give up when we do. He is not finished when we think he is. In fact, sometimes, he is just getting started when we think the need for prayer is over. Peter reminds us that God is not slow in keeping his promises because he has an eternal perspective (2 Peter 3:9). In fact, time simply serves his greater purposes of salvation. That is why, to

God, a day is like a thousand years and the reverse is true (2 Peter 3:8).

What do we need to possess to help us better understand how God uses time? Patience, perspective, and persistence are important if we are to ever understand how God works with and in time. If we can leverage these, we will be more likely to allow God to use time for our benefit.

Patience is necessary since we must realize that God does not function according to our timetable. We might be in a hurry. We usually are. I do not know of anyone who prays, "God, I really pray that you would do this for my family, but whenever is fine; no hurry here." Usually, if our loved one has cancer, we want it gone immediately. If the bill collectors are calling, we need resources now. If there is division in the family, we cannot bear another day of delay before reconciliation comes. If the job is to be filled soon, we immediately need to know if we got the job or not.

Now, patience as a concept involves time. Waiting is required, which is a response to time. Our biggest challenge is not feeling as though God is moving quickly. Millions of people wonder whether God is engaged at all, is listening, or is motivated to respond to our plight. Patience evaporates when we put God on our timetable.

I confess that I am not a patient person by nature. I have things mapped out. I know what needs to happen, how it should happen, and the time it should take for God to make it happen. I often wonder why God does not respond to my brilliant plan and do it with a sense of urgency. My plan has rationale, sequence, and logic to it. Some things are time sensitive. We invented the expression "time sensitive" for a reason. In my worst moments, I actually assume that I am more time sensitive than God is. He seems to have a more cavalier approach to what I consider urgent. How dare he? All my urging him in prayer does not seem to move the needle toward results as quickly as I believe it should. I am not alone on this. The prophet Habakkuk was wondering what was taking God so long to act upon the obvious evil in the nation of Judah. That nation was, after all, God's nation, his people. They should have behaved better and known better on at least a dozen fronts regarding how they should live. So, Habakkuk called out, "How long, LORD?" (Habakkuk 1:2). He gave reasons for his impatient desire to have matters addressed. He wanted God to act without delay. Habakkuk's prayer was similar to the sentiment of many other prophets.

Usually people impatiently want God to respond quickly, but sometimes people want God's patience to work in their favor. For instance, God may want an obedient response from me quickly on matters that I believe should not require an immediate response. However, if I am focused on a priority of mine when God places a nagging conviction in my spirit, I must do what he wants me to do before he will allow me to have a moment of peace or get back to my initial priority. We are fickle creatures to say the least. We want God to act immediately when it serves our purposes and be patient with us, giving us more time, when it comes to what he requires of us.

I remember one day when I was urgently trying to finish a sermon I was to present the next day. The whole while the phone would not stop ringing with emergencies from folks in the church and community. One of those emergencies was to walk a person back from a suicide attempt. Another one was a marriage in crisis and another was a desperate cry for help from a mother with a wayward child in legal trouble. I was able, by God's grace, to help in each case or steer the person to someone who could help better than me. Exasperated with all of the demands that stole my preparation time from me, I recall saying, "Okay, God, you have managed to allow my sermon preparation to be disrupted with all of these people in need. Now, I have no time to finish. It's on you." That is a stretch for me. I am a planner, and I was anxious without a plan. But according to many in the congregation the next day, my sermon was better than anything I usually prepared. The content was a sharp departure from what

I had planned. It was just what was needed in the church on that day. The time was spent doing things I did not feel were most important. There was no time for what I believed was important. God realigned my use of time as I redirected my commitments, filling in what was needed in lieu of my best efforts.

It is helpful to have a richer perspective of time and how God relates to it in order to allow him to do what only he can do: bring fulfillment to promises and shape us when we think the clock has struck midnight and all hope is gone.

Time, matter, space, and energy are constants in this world within which everything is enfolded. Matter and space are closely related and could be combined, but speaking in pedestrian terms, I will bifurcate them here. God is here and there (space). Most of us easily concede that God can be in all places simultaneously. Most adults can wrap their minds around that. God created all things (matter), and his sovereignty over it makes perfect sense. We understand it is his right to alter or influence matter. He can do whatever he wants with it since he created it. That is what happens for the most part in miracles. Seas are divided, sight is restored, and rains come at prophesied times. A vast majority of people in the world believe in miracles and believe that God can alter his creation as he pleases. Certainly, all Christians believe that God not only created stuff but authored and engineered life (energy). That makes perfect sense as well because God and absolute power are almost synonymous. The sun and its energy, as well as the breath in Adam and Eve, are all part of God giving life and distributing power.

Most Christians concede God's full right to exercise power over space, matter, and energy. No argument there. His manipulation of and exercise over them seem to be reasonable even if they provide some mental and philosophical challenges and would be strongly debated by those who do not believe. Anyone who believes there is a God must conclude that he has full reign over everything in his creation and under his control.

For some reason, most people cannot fathom how God

can manipulate time, subordinate it to his will, and make the most of it, though its objective qualities never seem to move or change. We have a problem understanding God's use of time. From our limited perspective, we somehow believe that if it looks as though something failed, and time has elapsed, thus rendering a solution impossible, then God has failed and missed his opportunity. Some people wonder if God is not somehow subject to the constraints of time just as we are. In other words, some of us think that God is held captive to time as we are. I have heard people say things like, "If God is going to do anything about this situation, he should hurry. Time is running out," or, "I prayed about this situation but God did nothing. I guess he did not hear me or has another plan for another time." That all assumes that time can run out on God and box him in just as it does us.

If we truly believe that God authored time as he authored matter, space, and energy, then we should believe that he can work in it, around it, through it, and beyond it. Our perspective of time should be that God is larger than time. Our understanding of subjective time should at least help us understand that God is not boxed in, bothered, or destined to fail if he does not do what we think he should in our prescribed time frame. Perhaps he is up to something bigger. Remember the idea of *pleroma*? He is unfolding greater results over time than we could imagine possible. Remember the notion of ripples and threads? God can take something that looks to be disconnected and make more of it. He does that with time. If we understand this, we might just be more patient with him. It is not over until God says it is.

That leads us to persistence. Patience is developed as we learn to wait for results, knowing that God is always at work. Persistence is our commitment to do the right things while we patiently wait. They are related. As such, persistence also helps us better understand time. Just keep doing what you know is right. Do not worry about time. If you do what is right, God will put the pieces together and make sense of it all. Time should not be a limiting factor to our obedience. However, I have seen that happen. I have watched people exercise great restraint for a period of time and then say, "Okay, I am done doing that. Patience hasn't produced the results I want." Time ultimately becomes more important to them than pleasing God. When we are not committed to persistently doing the right thing, time becomes the criteria for success and failure.

Persistence is that characteristic that says, "I will continue to do what is right whether it produces a result or not." It is a commitment to follow through even after the follow through has yielded disappointing results. Many people struggle with praying incessantly (1 Thessalonians 5:17). Their prayers only last as long as they believe there is still a predictable chance for success. When failure seems imminent or deadlines have expired, many people just stop praying. In those cases, prayer often changes and sounds defeated. Or when we have not received what we hope for, our prayer might be for plan B to develop. Persistence tells us that we will stay the course, doing the right things for the right reasons and not just for the desired results.

Persistence puts time in its place. It lets time know that it will not win the day. Time never runs out on persistence. We just continue to do what we know God wants us to do, stop when we get marching orders to stop, or to know that persistence itself demands that we change directions for the same reasons we continued the new course with the same vigor we had on the old one.

Patience, perspective, and persistence are fueled by faith. It is only in believing that God "exists and that he rewards those who earnestly seek him" (Hebrews 11:6) that we have the patience to wait for results. It is only when we have perspective that God can work, even when the prospects do not look good. Persistence leads us to do what needs to be done without allowing the results to destroy our energy or commitment. Faith in God moves us to please him and leave the results in his hands.

That should be our response to time. We should gain perspective, learn patience, and grow through persistence.

When faith is added to everything above, encouragement is sure to follow. Understanding that God works in, through, and above time becomes encouraging when we have faith that he is up to something good. Discouragement is more prevalent among those who lack faith. Faith, after all, is that quality that sees what is invisible. It carries assurance and certainty with it. It fails to ever say that it is over. Even when Jesus said, "It is finished," he was not indicating failure but completion of his mission. He spoke those words not just to mark an ending but also a beginning—the hope of salvation. His finished work gave us hope for more. Faith sees that more is coming even when things seem to be wrapping up.

Faith and time have an interesting relationship. Time tells us that all good things come to an end. In fact, time tells us that everything comes to an end. However, faith in God tells us that all good things will never come to an end. God is never done. Time reminds us that everything winds down and gets old, but faith reminds us that God makes all things new again (Revelation 21:5).

Faith is not oblivious of time. It is not. It is just not going to let time dictate final outcomes. Outcomes are entrusted to God and not settled by time's deadlines. Faith-filled people do not let time work against them, even if they come to the end of things here on earth. They acknowledge with the apostle Paul that whether prospects are grim or good things are prevalent, we are not fully clothed with what eternity has for us while we are here (2 Corinthians 5:1–4). That being the case, people of faith are not going to let time ruin their days along the way. That is what kept Jake DeShazer clipping along day after day, month after month, and year after year, even when time had run out on his fellow prisoners of war.

Bishop John Gollapalli is a friend of mine from India who happens to be a great leader. He and his lovely wife, Theeba, have done more good for people in need than most will ever come close to doing in a lifetime. They have developed schools, orphanages, livelihood training centers, and churches. They have influenced thousands of the poorest non-caste tribal people in India. Through their life-sustaining ministry (COUNT), they have managed to serve people with very few resources of their own. They have always trusted God to provide, and God has never failed them. They have rare faith and see exceptional results.

I have had the opportunity to be in their home and visit their ministry sites. Their accomplishments are nothing short of amazing. However, they would be quick to note that they have not done much. It has been God who has worked through them. Their demonstration of faith is inspiring. When I write these words about the relationship between time and faith, I think of them. They are always full of faith and never in a hurry. Trust me, they are never in a hurry. They understand that God will direct, provide, and move. I have never seen them panic, rush, push, or press to get results. That is not faith's way. It is not in them to operate that way. They just move forward and understand that time must submit to God just as they must submit to God. Their results are outstanding. I admire them and their deliberate trust in God that allows them to live at peace and walk at a pace that demonstrates they are waiting upon God.

Time is in God's hands. Faith should be in our hearts. When the two are rightly combined, the former never dictates the latter. Instead, faith understands that God will work things out no matter how loudly time screams and makes its demands known. But faith never sits back in the process; it moves forward in obedience.

If time is subject to God, and faith is in God's ability to leverage time in his own way, obedience is the commitment to put faith into practice regardless of what time dictates should be possible. Obedience is living out what we know to be right. It is not doing what we think is expedient or timely, but rather, doing what we know to be God's will. Obedience is acting in faith according to the truth. When we believe God and know his word to be true, we can do whatever he asks or commands without worrying about results or time.

Obedience is not a means to an end, but an end itself. That is confusing to some. I have heard people treat obedience like something we do in order to get to an expected outcome or a preferred result. That is like saying faith is trust in something for a period of time until we get tired of it or it does not produce what we want. That is not faith but something far less. Similarly, obedience is acting without regard for cost or outcome. It is faith tangibly exercised.

An immature approach to obedience is to treat it as a means to an end. Sometimes children think that if they do what their parents want (obedience) then they will get what they want (desire). Obedience as a means to an end says I will do it as long as it will get me what I want. However, obedience *as an end* is completely different and says I will do this because it is what God wants or expects of me. And if we do things simply because that is what God wants or expects of us, we often end up in the long run with much more than our feeble desires promise. Treating obedience as an end leads us to better results. However, if we are in a hurry, obedience will turn into expedience. When time gets involved with obedience, we can easily justify waiting for what God wants of us now.

Obedience, like its motivator—faith—has a relationship with time. Obedience does not allow time to have the final say. Time will not be the measure of obedience. In fact, obedience in its nature ignores time. It defers to God's will and lets the chips of time fall where they may whereas expedience allows time to dictate response.

As I mentioned, Marlene and I travel a lot. We have fellowshipped with believers in South America, Central America, Africa, the Middle East, Europe, Asia, Australia, and dozens of islands scattered throughout the seas of the world. We have friends in many of those countries and have lived in three of them. We have found that time-centric cultures generally have more money and resources and can accomplish a lot with their abundance of skills and other assets, but their personal lives are a little thin when it comes to staying the course and living lives of obedience to God. On the other hand, some of the countries that lack resources make up for it in an abundance of faith and obedience. After all, they often live in places where supplies are minimal, so trust becomes critical.

My friend John Gollapalli has always let his faith rather than time drive his obedience, and as a result, he has never let time dictate much of anything. Since he cannot make things happen, he allows God to make things happen and makes his concern to understand what that is and what he must do. That is obedience in its purest form.

I am not saying this is always the case in other cultures. It is often the case in countries where time is not of the essence since occupations, earning capacity, and deadlines are less prevalent. Time is not good as a primary motivator unless the motivation is our confidence in God's use of it. If we are confident that God will do what he sets out to do, we respectfully expect time to submit to God, just as we submit to him in obedience. Then the three (time, faith, and obedience) will work together and produce the results that God has in mind. That is why Isaiah prophetically quoted God saying, "It [my word] will not return to me empty, but will accomplish what I desire and achieve the purpose for which I sent it" (Isaiah 55:11). If we are confident that God's Word will not fail, then our faith and obedience to him and his Word is de facto confidence that, in time, God will do precisely what he said he would do. Time then becomes less our concern and more God's. Obedience becomes more our concern.

When time is submitted and placed in God's hands and we grasp faith and obedience in ours, we will finally receive the answers we have been looking for. We'll begin seeing results when we are less concerned about the results and more con-cerned about understanding God's will and responding to it.

When we seek God, time will seem to work for us. But when we seek answers with a deadline in mind, obedience and intimacy with God seems to allude us.

Personally, when I stop worrying about objective time and start focusing on doing what God wants me to do, I see more of his work taking place. I become more of the person I should be and learn how to wait patiently for God to answer. And he does.

King David was a man of action. He accomplished much in his life. He was productive as a musician, songwriter, king, shepherd, conqueror, servant of his predecessor, and much more. In fact, he was prolific and skilled in all of these roles. Yet, when it came to time, faith, and obedience, he could say:

> Trust in the LORD and do good; dwell in the land and enjoy safe pasture. Take delight in the LORD, and he will give you the desires of your heart. Commit your way to the LORD; trust in him and he will do this: He will make your righteous reward shine like the dawn, your vindication like the noonday sun. Be still before the LORD and wait patiently for him; do not fret when people succeed in their ways, when they carry out their wicked schemes. Refrain from anger and turn from wrath; do not fret—it leads only to evil. For those who are evil will be destroyed, but those who hope in the LORD will inherit the land. (Psalm 37:3–9)

It is clear that in order to end up in a good place, he needed to be still and wait patiently for God to act (Psalm 27:14). His words express that faith and obedience were his goals. Confidence in God to act was in his heart. I don't know of anyone who had more results and answers in their life than David. When he put time in God's hands, possessed faith, and exercised obedience in great measure, he saw results. Time placed in God's hands, and active faith and obedience carried out by our hands, results in a perspective that leads us to patience and persistence. When we live like that, time never runs out.

Project Me

- Reflect on a time when God urged you to act, but you chose to wait. How did the situation turn out? How would it have been different if you had acted immediately?

- Do you struggle with patience? Do you struggle with being too concerned with a schedule? Plan a schedule-free day with God. Ask him to determine your agenda for the day.

- Read all of Psalm 37. Reflect on David's life. What was it about David's life that allowed him to trust God without hesitation?

7

The Least Expected Places

Murphy's Law states that whatever can go wrong will go wrong. It implies that if there is a 99 percent chance you will arrive safely at your destination on time and a 1 percent that you will not, the odds are not good for a timely arrival. That always conjures a laugh from those of us who have had things go unpredictably wrong. It implies that the more important your appointment, the more likely something will arise to interrupt it. Of course, we all know that Murphy's Law is not something that actually occurs most of the time.

If I were to develop a mock law, I would go in a slightly different direction. I would call it the "Law of the Inverse Probability of Expectation versus Outcome." It would be defined as "the greater the expectation to find something where it is expected to be, the less likely it is that it will be there." Or conversely, "the least likely place you expect to find something to be is the most likely place you will find it." The older I get, the more this law is at work with me. It usually applies to the location of my keys, glasses, hat, and cell phone.

After nearly an hour of turning our house upside down looking for my keys in all the usual places, I once found them in the refrigerator crisper drawer. Of course, I should have started there—the least likely place to find keys. Apparently, I had them in my hand when I put a bag of veggies in the crisper after returning from the grocery store. They may have just hopped in there on their own when I wasn't looking. I guess that is a slight but unlikely possibility.

On another occasion, my cell phone was nowhere to be found. Again, I engaged in a thorough search of the whole house, between sofa cushions, every nook and cranny in my car, etc. Marlene obliged to call my number in an attempt to help me find it. We heard a faint ring coming from the trash can. Perhaps I should have expected it to be among the kitchen waste. I don't know how, but it ended up there somehow—the least likely place.

I have a friend whose hobby is finding treasures with a metal detector. He has found the strangest things in the most unsuspecting places. He told me that nothing surprises him anymore. How about when it comes to finding a parking spot when you need one the most, locating a friend in the place you would expect her to be, or coming up with the right word when people are listening?

As funny or sad as this may seem, there is some truth in it. At one time or another, everyone is surprised to find something where it does not belong or is not expected. Sometimes we are delightfully surprised to discover an unexpected benefit in an unexpected place. Some have made their greatest discovery or achievement in an accidental way (saccharin, Velcro, Play-Doh, the microwave oven, and penicillin were all accidents). Sometimes being lost ends up putting us in a providential setting. We may find ourselves in the wrong place, but unwittingly at the right time.

This happened to Marlene and me when we were on sabbatical in Europe. We were taking a full month visiting places we had yet to visit, backpacking with Eurail passes and no reservations. After visiting the sites in Florence, Italy (Uffizi Gallery, The Duomo, Piazza della Signoria, and other beautiful modern and ancient sites), we had a brilliant plan to get to the Cinque Terra for a few days on the Italian Riviera for rest and relaxation. Our bed and breakfast in Florence was a quaint local place where English was definitely not the language of choice. Actually, it was not spoken at all there. We were the only foreigners in the small hotel inhabited mostly by construction workers. When I asked which bus would get us back to the train station on the morning of our departure, the front desk clerk simply pointed in the direction of the bus stop. To minimize the need to speak, she only said, "29." Good enough. We had the general location and the bus number. What could go wrong?

We walked a couple of blocks down the road, saw some buses, noted one was 29A, and thought, *This is it*. We boarded and went for what seemed to be an interminably long ride. We skirted the city without ever entering it. I vaguely knew the way to the train station, but we were not going that way. People departed the bus over the course of the thirty-minute ride. Eventually the last passengers left at a stop. The driver turned off the bus and stepped off to have a smoke. We were obviously at the end of the line on the other side of Florence from where we boarded. I followed him out and said that we needed to go to the train station. Like the hotel clerk, he used the same amount of English saying, "29B." Needless to say, I was not thrilled. But we remained on the bus at his suggestion and rode for another twenty minutes back toward the city before we boarded another bus and arrived at the train station nearly ninety minutes late. I was frustrated, but Marlene cheerily said, "The Lord is up to something good." I love her optimism.

We missed the train we wanted and caught another train, which cascaded into more delays. Finally, catching a late afternoon train to the Cinque Terre, we ran and barely caught our last opportunity for a train. As we were running toward our designated train car, I heard someone say, "Pastor Matt?" I turned and saw a young couple I knew from our hometown in the United States. The young man had worked in our youth group for years and had moved away, married, and started a career elsewhere. We sat together with Joel and Amy on the train and had the most delightful ride and visit. Marlene turned to me and said, "See? The Lord was up to something." I am not implying that every mistake ends up with wonderful outcomes. I am implying that we should not be so surprised when they do.

The Bible is full of examples of those ending up in the least expected places or circumstances. For instance, Moses was a fugitive who fled from Egypt. But God sent him back to the least likely place of his greatest impact—Egypt. God gained the greatest impact through Moses, as he did nearly all Bible heroes, in the least suspected places and least expected ways.

Joseph was an annoyance to his brothers because he was clearly his father's favorite (Genesis 37:3). His brothers did their best to get rid of him. When they could not agree on whether to murder him or leave him for dead in a cistern, they chose a less morbid and more beneficial way of disposing of him. They sold him to foreigners headed to Egypt who would likely sell him into slavery there, knowing that would make him as good as dead but also line their pockets a bit without the guilt of killing their kin (37:28). With a dusting of the hands they likely said to one another, "There! We will never see him again." Au contraire!

They not only saw him again, but he also saved them in more than one way. He played a bigger part in their lives in the end than he did in the beginning (Genesis 42–48). Instead of being rid of him, they became dependent upon him. He cared for them, even though they tried to dispose of him. They found themselves in the least likely place that they could have imagined years before. They reconnected, not as enemies but as friends, and in an entirely different and redeemed relationship. Who could have imagined?

Similarly, Jacob thought he would never see Esau again,

and if he did, he thought it would be in combat. They too reconnected as brothers and friends.

David was the runt of his family and destined to be a harp-playing shepherd. He could not have dreamed of being the most influential king in Israel's storied history, with his name appearing throughout the Bible.

The last place on earth Jonah wanted to be was Nineveh, but there he was—after spending several days in the belly of a great fish. His mission field was Nineveh, like it or not.

Haman had every intention to build gallows for his archenemy, Mordecai, and plot the destruction of Mordecai's people. Instead, he brought destruction on himself on his own gallows.

Daniel wanted nothing of politics and just wanted to be left alone to attend to his devotion to God. Yet he became the most influential political figure next to the king of Babylon.

There were prophets who had no aspirations for prophecy, heroes who never viewed themselves as such, inconspicuous poor people who never thought God could use them, and widows who would have never imagined their story would be told for millennia to come. In each case, these folks would have said that their place of greatest influence was the least likely place they could have imagined. And the situation becomes even more pronounced in the New Testament. The Christian with the greatest potential to impact the nation of Israel was Saul (later named Paul). He was admittedly from the right tribe and had the right pedigree, character, and training to influence the nation of Israel. He spoke the language, had earned the respect of his peers, and knew all the right people. But what did God do with this Israeli-leader-turned-Christian? He sent him to be among an entirely different race of people who were not at all impressed by his credentials or heritage. God told him the first week of his conversion, without consultation or warming him up, that he would become a missionary to the Gentile world (Acts 9:15). In other words, God was calling him to reach the people he was least fond of and who would be least impressed with his credentials.

If there was ever a questionable call in the Bible, it would be this one. Paul had ample knowledge to help him reach his own people. He even shared their disdain for Christians, which would have given him a way into their inner circles. He knew the arguments against Christianity from the Jewish angle and could argue them flawlessly. After his conversion, he could now refute them with equal aplomb, but God commissioned him into ministry to largely Gentile or mixed churches (Acts 13:1–3) alongside a hodge-podge of Jewish and Gentile missionaries.

Paul's training seemed to be a waste. Every time he tried to minister to his own people, it turned out to be a disaster (Acts 13:50; 14:19; 17:5). Despite his repeated efforts to reach everyone—Jews and Gentiles (Acts 13–17)—he finally concluded that it was a waste of time and effort for him to attempt to reach his own people. He finally announced that he had had it and was not going to attempt to reach his own people despite his qualifications (Acts 18:6) and desire to do so. This whole outcome confuses theologians to this day. What seemed to be the brightest opportunity turned out to be a largely ineffective endeavor. What seemed to be the least likely place for effective ministry turned out to be the best.

Why God did not use an insider to reach insiders defies leadership theory. An endeavor often finds its greatest potential where the people involved have skill, experience, and passion. Surprisingly, Paul was arguably the most effective missionary in the most unlikely place to the most incompatible people in history. On top of that, Paul suffered terribly as he took on the ministry for which he was the least qualified.

Who would then reach the Jewish nation? God had that covered as well with—you probably guessed it by now—the least qualified person to reach the Jews. Peter had been someone very close to Jesus, but very far away from any respectable position that would command respect from respectable Jews.

He had no pedigree, little formal training, and had demonstrated cowardice in times when it mattered to have the backbone he'd need to reach a hostile people (Luke 22:54–62). These people had no respect for Peter's trade or his qualifications (Acts 4:13). They were not at all impressed and allowed him no voice to speak (Acts 4:18). However, as easily dissuaded as he was before Jesus' arrest and trial, denying that he even knew Jesus, he was committed to stumbling and bumbling through preaching the gospel to people who would not listen, guided by the power of the Holy Spirit (Acts 4:19–20; 23–31).

I am sure that given the examples above, Peter would have responded with all of the famous prophets, kings, apostles, and leaders of the Bible. Peter probably never expected saying something like, "I never saw that coming. I would not have guessed in a million years that I would be effective where God placed me." That is just the way God uses people—in the least likely ways and in the least likely places. The least likely places turn out to be the most likely places for effective ministry.

One could even look at Jesus Christ. The place of his greatest work on our behalf (our salvation) was not worked out in his eternal home but as a stranger on the earth. He entered our world, took on our sin, and redeemed our lives, making us his family—all while living far from home. He was in the least likely place but had the greatest impact. He was an outcast in this environment that we call home. Ironically, his status as an outcast afforded him the opportunity to transform this world inside out even while divesting himself of some power and influence. He restrained himself, making his lasting impact seem like even more of a stretch. God the Father used Jesus' restraint to increase his Son's exposure to us, or, more accurately, our exposure to him. The contrast of his presence in the world that rejected him was necessary to complete his effective work for us. Oddly, none of this took place in his eternal residence; rather, it took place in our temporal one. The least likely places somehow become the way God works.

So, why not us? Why not now? What would make us think that God would start doing things differently than he did throughout the Bible? Most people think that God should or will use them in the places where they feel most comfortable and useful and effective—the places where we feel adequate and capable and can take the credit for our own success. We tend to assume that if God knew what he was doing, he would use us in places where the likelihood of our success seems guaranteed. He never did that in the Bible and will not likely start now. We tend to think that if God knew what he was doing, then he would use us in places where the likelihood of our success is more pronounced. But why would he?

God is not going to let that happen; he would prefer that we depend upon him. He prefers the shock value of working against the odds. God wants us to experience dependence upon him, which allows him to do the extraordinary and miraculous. The most likely places are too predictable. When God wants our attention and full obedience, he uses us in places where reliance upon him is a must.

We get a window into God's methodology and rationale in this regard in Judges 6 and 7. As always, God worked against the odds in these chapters on purpose. God called Gideon to defeat an intimidating army. What makes this outstanding is that Gideon was the least likely person from the least important family, which was part of the least impressive clan in the least notable tribe of Israel (Judges 6:11–16). It is almost comical how God works upside down in this situation. He calls and relies upon the most insignificant person to do the biggest job.

That is not all. When Gideon tried to qualify his efforts by amassing a substantial fighting force of 32,000 people, God made him reduce his men to just 10,000 (Judges 7:3). But even that was too many and too likely for success in God's eyes. The fighting force was not small enough yet. So, God conducted another exercise to reduce the army to the least likely size possible (Judges 7:4–8). The final fighting group was a measly 300.

That was a reduction of 31,700 fighting men. Gideon was the least likely person in the least likely place with the least likely army. Again, that is how God does things.

God gave Gideon and the readers of his story a window into the rationale of his small person and small army strategy, paring down along the way to fight the battle. He told Gideon, "You have too many men for me to deliver Midian into their hands. In order that Israel may not boast against me that her own strength saved her" (Judges 7:2). The implication is that God did not want anyone thinking that Gideon or the people won the victory by their own strength. He did not want them to think that their strength was the deciding factor. He did not want the people to glory in their own strength, but in God's power. That's it. God really wants to use the least likely in the least likely way.

It is not that God wants to use us to make a point to the world. He wants to make a point to us, and through us as well. He wants us to exert our faith in places where God needs to show up in tangible ways so he gets the credit for our successes. He uses us in the least likely places as a standard order of things. It increases our dependence upon him. It increases our need to pray to him and seek his strength and wisdom.

When and where you feel least qualified might just be the place and time that God uses you most significantly. Do not shy away from a calling that seems difficult or frightening. That is the way God works most often and most powerfully. As his project, he wants to complete us by allowing us to experience utter dependence upon him. That is his consistent method. It is never our preferred method.

This principle has played out again and again in my life. I have spent time (or what I would rather call wasted time) with people, in places, and around situations where I questioned why I would even bother to work. Many times I have questioned why God had me in a particular place with particular people or in a particular circumstance when it seemed like someone else could do better. Without any sense of understanding or qualification, I would look at the situation as time poorly spent. In the end, those instances turned out to be some of the most productive relationships, places, and ministry opportunities of my life.

I "wasted my time" while I was pastoring a growing church. The wasted time was with a shy fifteen-year-old youth. God made it clear to me that I should spend time discipling this boy who came from a hostile home environment. That boy later became a leader of a national ministry that produces incredible fruit. I also "wasted my time" visiting repeat offenders in prison who had succumbed to generational cycles of violence and crime. On at least two occasions, those efforts, which seemed to be charity endeavors at best, turned out to produce powerful and impactful ministry leaders. In fact, the most significant things I remember happening in my life were connected in some way to times, places, or people that I least expected to be potentially fruitful.

Through the years, I have suggested that people should refrain from telling God that there is no way or that they wouldn't be able to do that. I have met effective missionaries, pastors, political leaders, business entrepreneurs, and ministry leaders who have told me that at one time or another, when they sensed God leading them in the direction of their greatest success, they laughed or smugly said, "No way!" That seems to be a common experience. An almost universal maxim is that whatever you do, do not tell God that you won't or can't when he calls you. Similarly, I have heard people say, "If you want to make God laugh, tell him your plans." Our plans usually contain places, activities, and relationships where we feel most qualified. They are places where we can predict success and receive credit. That is not God's way.

But God is all about tapping into the unexpected. Years ago, a massive tsunami devastated Thailand, Indonesia, Sri Lanka, India, and other countries. Thousands died as a result. The thousands of churches in our ministry family were asked to make contributions toward relief and rebuilding. Money came in. Tens of thousands of dollars were raised, mostly in America and Canada. But it was not enough to address the overwhelming need of all the members and churches in our own ministry family, much less everyone else who was affected. We made some global appeals and received generous but limited gifts. One gift stood out. It was a gift from our leaders in Haiti, one of the poorest countries in the world. An appeal went out from our leaders there to the members of our churches there, telling them that their suffering brothers and sisters on the other side of the globe needed their help. Dozens of churches participated. In that country, where the majority of the population at that time lived on less than three US dollars per day, the gift was small. If I remember correctly, it was $218. We had already dispersed significant amounts. This gift was not even enough to repair the roof of a small home.

I happened to share the story of their generosity with people in the United States, Asia, and around the world. I was personally blessed by this small but sacrificial gift, so I shared their story. I did not share it to prime the pump for giving or even to applaud any specific individual in Haiti or their leadership. I was just sharing what I perceived to be a blessing, knowing the sacrifice and love that accompanied the gift. It was not the amount but the love from which it came. I did not take an offering or make an appeal from that story. But, after sharing their story, tens of thousands of dollars did come flooding into our crisis response fund from which relief money was drawn. In fact, more money came in after that story became known than before. In a real sense, that least-likely-to-benefit-anyone gift became the catalyst for the flood of resources we were able to dispatch to help hundreds and hundreds of people. The least of the gifts became the greatest! That may sound very familiar to anyone familiar with the words of Jesus (Luke 9:48).

This experience is not an anomaly. It is our calling. We become complete when we allow God to use our experiences of weakness and inadequacy to impact the world and make us into useful servants. Don't tell God that you are unqualified, unless you are prepared to hear him say that you are the perfect vessel for what he wants you to accomplish.

Project Me

- When's the last time you lost something and it seemed to take forever to find it? Where did you end up finding it? How did you feel after you found it?

- This chapter is included in the book because the project that God is working to complete is *you*. He wants to use you to get things done. Where might God want to use you today, tomorrow, and in the future?

- Think of a time when you gave a small gift that impacted many. Or think about a time when you were given what many might see as a small gift, but to you it had a great impact. Reflect on that. Consider that no gift, act, or prayer is small when it is backed by God's direction.

8

Redemption, Restoration, and Recycling

Redemption is one of our language's sweetest and most emo-
tionally moving words. We use the term all the time in ordinary
ways. We talk about redeeming a discount with a coupon, cash-
ing in a gift card, or buying something that had been pawned.
Redemption in those terms is nice, but nothing significant or
moving. They are just functional transactions. There is nothing life
transforming in that usage. Redemption, as it relates to a human
life, is much sweeter. It is transformational. It is emotion-inducing
and life-changing.

I have been in places where the ministries I help lead are
involved in redemption all the time. I have visited safe houses
where girls who had been trafficked as sex slaves have been
redeemed from abuse and inhumane treatment and from people
who used them and caused unimaginable harm. They have been
redeemed and now live lives where love, community, and dignity
are the daily norm. Those girls are not coupons or gift cards.
They are living, breathing people made in God's image who
have been salvaged from the trash heap of discarded humanity.

That kind of redemption is the reclaiming of a life all but lost or destroyed and made whole again. Those beautiful women and girls are well on their way to recovery and discovering God's original purpose and design for them in a loving community.

I have conversed with men, women, and children who have recounted the abuse they suffered at the hands of radical terrorist groups in the Middle East. Those terrorists have done unbelievable harm. The level of abuse is too horrible to mention. After walking for days with no clothing, food, or water, they find safe haven with some of the churches I serve. Their basic needs are cared for, and they are loved and embraced as children of God. Because of that love and acceptance, scores of them are becoming followers of Jesus and learning to receive the love of God. They are redeemed from the most despicable human behavior and given the opportunity to live lives of love, purpose, and hope. That kind of redemption is more than exchanging a coupon for a free toy. It is redemption from death to life.

God is our Redeemer (Psalm 78:35; Isaiah 44:6, 24; 1 Peter 1:18). He redeems humanity. Jesus offers redemption to those who believe in him (Titus 2:13; Galatians 3:13–14). Redemption language is prevalent throughout the Bible occurring more than one hundred times. It makes perfect sense that God would do that. As Creator, he made us. As Redeemer, he alone can reclaim what is broken or lost. He is the original Maker and the only Redeemer. Since he alone designed us, he alone can reclaim us and buy us back. But he does so without money (Isaiah 52:3). Jesus did it with his own life.

This is more than a concept. It is a description of what God does to and for us. It is the story of how we can come back to him and to our created purpose. He takes that which was lost and brings it back. The imagery in the Bible is dramatic: lost sheep brought back, lost sons returning home, lost coins found—all referring to the work of redemption. The imagery also includes references to our own enslavement. We were slaves to sin. God redeems us from a life of our own enslavement of lower desires and self-destruction. In the case of most of us, it is not redemption from traffickers but from sin. God redeems us from that which we are powerless to redeem ourselves.

Redemption is at the core of salvation. It is buying back, reclaiming from the landfill or refuse pile, that which had value at one time but was damaged or lost and making it valuable once again. This concept is at the center of most sermons in churches as it should be. That is the essential work upon which we depend. We need God to redeem us. We need him to take that which is broken and make it whole again—to buy us back from the enslavement we have been too quick to allow. We need God to remake us and reverse satan's damage. Redemption is sweet when it occurs. It is taking something that has been reduced to nothing and making it more than we could ever think imaginable (1 Corinthians 1:26–30). Jesus is our righteousness, holiness, and redemption—all sweet terms that put us back where we were made to be.

Once we are redeemed, restoration can take place. Restoration is a sweet word as well. It is the result of our journey back to what we were made to be. Restoration is the remaking of a redeemed life. Restoration is a work in itself. If redemption is the work of salvation, restoration is the work of sanctification. It is remaking us in God's own image—the image in which we were originally created. Once bought back (redeemed) from the trash pile, the work of cleaning off, fixing up, and making new again (restoration) is God's persistent, sanctifying work that continues until we are fully complete. Redemption is buying something back. Restoration is making it work again as intended.

I like fixing things. I am not good at it, but I enjoy it. It feels good to make something useful again. Whether it is fixing a leaking pipe, a broken toy, or sanding down rust and refinishing the car with paint, restoration brings a certain satisfaction. Usually when I fix something, it is clear that it has not been done by a professional. It usually looks tarnished. The colors might not match perfectly. The shape may be a little off. But hey, it works!

I know some people who are very good at restoration. One friend of mine is constantly buying cars and restoring them. When he is finished with them, they look and work better than new. I admire his skill but do not relate to it very well. However, anyone who does that work feels a level of satisfaction since the thing being restored has usefulness and beauty once again.

Restoration is the critical part that follows redemption. It is the laborious work done with those in refugee camps or victims of enslavement and abuse. Redeeming young girls from sex trafficking can be done in a matter of days. It is usually done at great risk and requires legal help and covert recovery efforts. Once redeemed, the very long, hard, and painful work of restoration begins. Abuse victims continue to fear the possibility of more abuse, and their restoration requires a compassionate approach and a commitment to build trust. The restoration process includes lots of love, care, education, and vocational training. It mandates a community of people committed to help, mentor, love, and accept both the victims and their sometimes defensive behavior.

Many of the girls who have been sold into slavery were sold by their own parents or guardians who are all too willing to sell them again if given the opportunity, which is why the restoration process requires both protection from all who wish to harm them and a rebuilding process committed to helping families resolve their relational dysfunctions and financial hardships. Restoration is hard and complex. It takes years, if not a lifetime.

The same is true of restoration for refugees who have fled from their country of origin. They have left their family, culture, language, home, friends, and familiar surroundings. They have generally left all their belongings or what little they had. The work of restoration entails rebuilding their entire life in an unfamiliar environment with people who have not yet earned their trust. What has amazed me about the refugees I've worked with from Africa and the Middle East, where I have seen the refugee situation the most, is how resilient they are. God has given remarkable resilience that is miraculous.

From my perspective, the resilience of refugees who have been severely traumatized or scarred and had their entire family murdered or enslaved is just as miraculous as witnessing a lame person walking again. To see refugees' wounds (physical, emotional, relational, mental, and spiritual) healed and turned into healthy scars is nothing short of amazing. In many cases, when I witness the work of restoration, it leaves me speechless. I met a young man from Central Africa who had walked for days after he witnessed the slaughter of his whole family and village. While the massacre, which saw his whole village destroyed, was occurring, he pulled two dead bodies on top of himself and feigned death for hours until it was finally over. It was dusk before the small but heavily armed band of soldiers left his village. Under cover of night, that young man took some provisions, fled the area, walked for days, and arrived at a refugee camp in the Democratic Republic of Congo.

He told me of his experience in a very matter-of-fact way over cake and coffee in the foyer of the church he attends in the United States, where he had settled. He showed me scars from the gunshot and knife wounds he received on that fateful day as a fifteen-year-old. His pain seemed to be dimly present but was overshadowed by the restored health, peace, and love given by God and affirmed by God's family. The pain of the past was overshadowed by his smile, laughter, and joy. The internal work of God in his life through the ten years since his escape is nothing less than astounding. Restoration is the unbelievably encouraging work of God.

As with redemption, many sermons and teachings in the church focus on restoration. They should. Redemption is reclaiming life. Restoration is rebuilding it. These get the attention they should receive. But there is another work that often gets ignored. It is a necessary component to the process of God's work to complete us: recycling.

The recycling work of God is what this book is mostly about. If redemption is reclaiming the lost and restoration is making it new again, recycling is using the experiences along the way for other purposes. God will repurpose all our relationships and experiences again and again to bring wholeness to us and others along our life journey. It is God who repurposes our experiences. Sometimes that repurposing includes sharing our stories in ways that inspire others to faith. Sometimes God recycles our experiences to help others understand what redemption and restoration look like. Sometimes God recycles our experiences to bring encouragement to others or increase our patience and endurance for other matters. Every experience in life should be referenced, remembered, or retold for the future benefit and blessing of others. I have seen many people recycle their physical, emotional, and relational scars into testimonies of God's grace. It has been said that the best sign of a good healer is a healthy scar. The scar itself is the opportunity to relive or retell what has happened as a sign that healing has taken place.

Recycling entails using something repeatedly instead of just once. In the commercial sector, the concept of recycling discarded plastic, metal, glass, and paper has only been around for a few generations. Now we have an understanding that we can save energy, reuse materials over and over again, decrease waste, and save money by recycling. Even though some folks still do not see the value in it, so they discard whatever they use after that one use. Overall, however, recycling has captured the imagination of a generation that is interested in conservation and stewardship of the earth and its resources.

I wish people knew how God desires to recycle our experiences and use them again and again for our own future experiences, the benefit of others, and the building of the world around us. It would be a shame for an experience that benefitted us greatly to go to waste. Instead, it should be stored up and ready for reuse in the future to encourage others. God wants to maximize every experience. He has the ability to take one experience and reproduce good from it over and over again.

Jesus did not pour his life into his disciples for three years for their benefit only. He also fully expected them to recount their experiences, not only for their own mutual encouragement but also for the benefit of everyone all over the world who knew and lived out what that first generation knew and were living out. Jesus would have spent far more than three years on earth if the initial experience would have been all he expected to produce from his time on the earth. If he thought that the sum total of his efforts was for the groups he impacted, it would be safe to assume he would have spent a good fifty years here teaching, healing, saving, and correcting. Instead, he just needed three years with the apostles to ensure that they knew him and understood who he was and what he had come to do. He only needed to die once for their salvation. After his resurrection, he only needed to be raised from the dead for a short period of time before ascending to heaven to communicate with them and give the physical assurance that he conquered death. He didn't need years.

Instead, he expected the benefits from his life, death, and resurrection to be applied repeatedly, and not only for that generation and group of friends but for every generation and people all over the world for centuries to come. He knew he needed to have enough experiences with the disciples for the stories to be written down and subsequently recounted over and over again for millennia. He prayed that many would believe based on the testimony of these intimate friends of his (John 17:18–23). He knew that we would be able to live similarly throughout our lives and be a community of people living in unity just as he had done with his friends. Jesus fully expected their experiences to be recycled, retold, repackaged, and redistributed in thousands of languages to billions of people. He expects no less from us. He expects our experiences to be recycled, retold, repackaged, and redistributed as well.

The apostles' experiences were to be reviewed, remembered, relived, and retold. The recycling work of taking their experience for the benefit of others resulted in the formation of the New Testament. In that record, we can benefit over and over from the stories told and written. We can relive the miracles, appreciate the teachings, and be challenged to a life of obedience.

Some of the recycling of the apostles' experiences come at the expense of their dignity. The apostles did not shy away from sharing about their selfish and competitive spirit. They were not reluctant to share about their preoccupation with their own egos. They did not hesitate to tell how patient Jesus was with their doubt-filled antics when he was still alive. Why? Why would they subject themselves to humiliation for future generations to retell? They sincerely wanted their experiences to be known so others would benefit from them. They wanted to warn people about the dangers of ego and selfishness. They did not neglect telling about pushing children away from Jesus or trying to get people to leave them alone. Peter narrated the very passages that would implicate him as a Jesus denier. He told his story so everyone would know that caving under pressure can happen to the best of us. Peter wanted his experience to be recycled for our benefit.

The apostles initially hid in a closed room to keep from being discovered after Jesus' death on the cross. Their experience was theirs alone. Their relationship with Jesus was theirs alone. I am certain that they did not see the long-term need to share their experiences with others, even though Jesus told them that they must. They likely had the initial mindset that their experiences would benefit them alone in the future. I am sure they had no clue how their experiences would be recycled for their own growth and the salvation of the world. Gradually, they saw their experiences as something to serve as instruction, encouragement, and warning for the world around them. That is why they were eager to write everything down and travel far and wide to teach a new generation to live in obedience to Jesus. Their three years with Jesus launched a lifetime of blessings and benefits to others.

I wish we could all realize that our momentary difficulties, temporary experiences, and short-term relationships will have a lasting benefit and use when it comes to God building up ourselves and others. We should be able to learn from those experiences repeatedly. If we understand their power, we will be less prone to forget them and more intentional about remembering them. We can weave those stories together with other relationships and experiences to piece together a more complete tapestry of life. The narrative of our lives will grow and become clearer as God recycles our experiences. We must simply be prepared to be surprised at how our experiences are recycled for future benefit.

Most of the time, our experiences go unnoticed or disregarded as single moments in time, reflecting little on our future. They often come back as examples to help us know what to do, what not to do, how to respond, or how not to respond. If we forget them, they are of little value. If we learned nothing from the lessons from previous experiences, we will likely learn nothing from the repeat experiences.

That is why I recommend journaling. Chronicling the accounts of your life, especially those unusual events that seem out of place or difficult to understand, helps us make sense of that which seems odd or unwelcomed. It forces us to think about each event more deeply. A journal can serve as our memory when our memory is faint and unreliable, and writing things down gives us opportunity to record our emotions and responses to what was going on for comparative purposes should we ever experience the events again. It helps us categorize and compare experiences. Our journal entries can remind us of people who walked with us during those times too. As such, it helps us remember to call upon or thank those who have traveled the journey with us. The benefits of journaling are endless. Recycling only works if we remember and can retell. Sadly, most people just experience life in the moment and hope to forget their odd or unwelcomed experiences—the very thing we should not do. The more unusual the experience, the greater the likelihood that it will serve us in the future.

When my family lived in Asia, I had a very unusual experience, and have never experienced anything like it since. Bernice called me early one morning with panic in her voice. Her family had worked for years to afford a Jeepney, a popular style of bus in the Philippines, that serve as the primary instrument in their business and was critical to their livelihood (transporting bananas, coconuts, and other fruits to the market from the farm). Her son and his cousin were the licensed drivers who transported things to the city.

They had not returned from their work the previous day. Bernice and her husband did some investigating and discovered that some corrupt people had stolen their vehicle, sold it, and accused the young owners of some outlandish things that landed her son and nephew in jail and allowed them to steal and keep their vehicle. The police were holding them in jail without bond, and they were awaiting a trial that might never take place. Things looked bleak for the young men who were just doing their job and were taken advantage of by cunning criminals.

Bernice appealed to me, begging for my help. I did not know what to do, so I called a respected attorney who was a member of the church I served. He informed me that this kind of thing unfortunately happened in that area often and there was likely nothing we could do. He advised me to stay out of it for my own safety and the safety of my family. He informed me that this was part of an organized crime ring that had pervasive influence throughout the city.

Prompted in prayer, I knew I could not possibly just sit and watch this injustice take place. I went to the jail where the young men were held. I appealed to the police to let me see them. They refused. I asked (probably "demanded" is more accurate) to see the officer in charge. Surprisingly, they summoned him, and he approached me. He was stern, and I quickly discerned that he was not going to accommodate my request to see or release the young men into my care. I did not know what to do and used a few legal terms, the most applicable being "habeas corpus." I also noted that I planned to file a complaint asking for a trial, and that the unlawful detainment of these young men would result in penalty to all parties responsible for their arrest and incarceration. I went even further and said that I was planning to call the United Sates embassy in that country to note this occurrence and do whatever I could to point out the pattern of behavior, suggesting they would file a complaint on my behalf with the local and national government.

I did not want to reference the local attorney I spoke with since he was less than enthused about my involvement in the first place and any mention might endanger him or his family. I knew no other attorneys in that city. I did, however, reference a powerful attorney in America (John), who had won many cases against unjust activities. I did not know if that would even make a difference in the mind of the local police. But I thought I would put it out there and follow up if needed. It was a desperate attempt to secure the release of these young men. I was throwing John's name out there in desperation, hoping that if I called him, he would respond and help even though he had no jurisdiction or claim to practice law in that country. I doubted there was anything he could do.

To my surprise, the officer in charge responded by releasing the young men to me and said that no charges would be filed. The vehicle was not released, and it was sadly a lost cause. But at least the young men were free! I did not need to contact my attorney friend since the matter was over in less than an hour. The parents were delighted and tearfully grateful for the young men's release. The story seemed to be over, but it was worthy of writing it down in my journal.

Years later, upon returning to the United Sates, I read my

journal again and was reminded of the incident. I recounted it to a friend over lunch who happened to know John, the attorney I'd briefly considered calling. Without my knowing, he passed the word on to John. A week or two later, I received a bill in the mail on official letterhead from a law firm. When I opened it, I saw a bill for $5,000. I was in shock. I had not contracted any legal services from any law firm. My heart sank. He had his office send services rendered in absentia. As I gasped, I read a handwritten note at the bottom of the bill with a smiley face, and I realized it was a joke. It read, "Glad I could help. Use my name anytime. Welcome back to the US."

John and I reconnected over lunch, and he subsequently became a Christian. He opened relational doors with his friends and family where I could share about the ministry. The end result was the unsuspecting support of our ministry. He also helped expand my relationships in the legal community in my home city. What I perceived to be an effort to benefit two young men and a desperate mother in one country led to their release and later an open door for ministry in another country many years later. God recycled my overseas experience that I would have discarded as a one-and-done event.

Words, conversations, experiences, and relationships can be, and likely will be, recycled if we understand that God works in layers and completes us with what seems to be random, disconnected pieces. God redeems and reclaims that which was lost. God restores. He rebuilds what was broken. Most people of faith understand that, but many forget that God also recycles. He brings back to the surface those conversations, experiences, and relationships that we have long since forgotten. He turns them into useful tools for future building and benefit. Nothing is lost unless we lose it. Nothing is useless unless we render it so. Nothing is forgotten unless we forget it. God does not lose, consider useless, or forget anything. He is looking for more places to allow our valuable experiences to resurface.

Project Me

- When was the last time you fixed something? After you fixed it, how did the sense of accomplishment make you feel?

- It's time to recycle! What aspect of your personality could use some recycling? If you cannot think of anything, ask a trusted accountability partner or your spouse. Like the apostles, we can all use some recycling, even if it costs us a bit of our dignity.

- Do you keep a journal? If not, it's time to start one. Today, spend time journaling about a recent conversation that had an impact on you. If appropriate, reconnect with that individual.

PART 2 SUMMARY

Life is not a series of disconnected events. The conversation you had this morning impacts the lives of those involved for years to come, whether it seems consequential or not. Traumatic events, peculiar engagements, and delightful celebrations all leave imprints for years to come. Stories and experiences of them may even resurface many times over. When they do, they add to our wisdom in making decisions, our patient understanding of others, and help us be appropriately cautious regarding how we proceed with relationships and decisions for tomorrow.

God is great and has the ability to script, shape, remake, and reuse our experiences in ways that we will never understand and most often never see. We only see the tip of the iceberg. The impact of our lives spills over to countless others, and God uses it all for blessing, teaching, and maturing. Again, God is not a capricious Lord or a disinterested puppet master. He is engaged at such a profound level that every ounce of our lives can be used to shape the world around us.

Too many experiences are wasted or ignored by too many

people. They are looked at as bizarre intrusions into our ordered world. They are not, and should not be, viewed as such. Instead, we should be filled with curiosity as we wonder how our experiences will resurface and impact our lives in the future. I often pray, "God, thank you for guiding me through this experience. Please use it for my growth and wisdom, for your glory and for the edification of others for years to come." I find myself telling people who minimize their remarkable experiences that they should write a book, or at least write it down. The story has not ended yet. The best chapters are yet to come.

It is good to know that God is working in ways we cannot see. Is there, however, a way we can get a better glimpse of what God is doing in our lives and how it should impact us daily? In part 3, we will look at how the pieces are put together as the project God is working on is lived out in real time. We will live differently when we realize that God uses it all.

Part 3

My Part in the Project

9

Looking Through and Beyond

Luke, our son, is intelligent, creative, industrious, hardworking, and thrifty. He is that way at work as a teacher, in his hobbies, at home, and with his family. His wife, Jennifer, is the perfect match on every level, possessing those attributes and many others. Luke applies all those virtuous qualities to the endless sea of home projects they start and complete. He is much better at home improvement projects than I am.

One Saturday, Luke asked if I was available to help him set some new windows. He did all the prep work, removing the old windows and getting the framing set. I was there to assist, measure, shim, place, insulate, and trim as we installed the new windows. Easy enough. What I lack in creativity, I make up for in intensity and focus when I'm following directions. I am one focused individual. If painting by number is a real art form, call me an artist. So, we measured, leveled, tacked, and did the rest. I looked intently at each window and we made sure everything was flush with the wall and square with the house. I cleaned stickers and other debris from the windows after they were set, admiring our work and complementing the excellent work of my son, the project chief.

We were only one window shy of completing the project when Jennifer entered the room with some lunch she had prepared. We pulled up some chairs near the window, and talked, laughed and visited while his children ran in and out of the room and we enjoyed lunch. Luke looked out the window we had just set, pointing out some features on the hillside across the way. He showed me where deer made their paths up and down the hill. He pointed out some trees where unusual species of birds would frequent as they migrated through the area. Luke and Jennifer are serious bird watchers. In that moment, it dawned on me that for the first time all day I was actually looking through the window, beyond the panes themselves.

I realized that I had spent the whole morning looking at the windows rather than through them. Don't get me wrong—my job was to look at them not through them. I would have been of little help if I had spent the whole time admiring the view. My role in that moment was not to enjoy the view but to make sure the windows were properly set. Again, I am a focused person. I am intent on doing what needs to be done. The job that day was not to treat the window as a window but as a project to complete. However, the real purpose and function of windows is not to be viewed as a project, but a way to see the world. Their purpose is to provide a view of the outside world and allow light to come into the house.

While having lunch, I captured a glimpse of one of humanity's biggest problems. We spend far too much time looking "at" and "near," rather than "through" and "beyond." We look at the problem, event, or circumstance, rather than through it to what it might become. We tend to focus on a problem, event, or circumstance rather than beyond to the implications and contributions they make. I fully understand that when we are in the midst of living life, our job is to make sure things are done well and respond wisely. For instance, when we're setting windows, in the moments of construction, we need to look at the event. But at some point, we must take a longer look than we do in analyzing the event itself. We must look to what this might mean for our future.

If Luke and Jennifer hadn't pointed out the view from the window we'd just installed, I am certain I would have left their house with a more limited understanding of their neighborhood and the world around them. It would not have dawned upon me to look through and beyond. As a result, I would have missed a key moment with my family, enjoying the view, our relationship, and the world that God created to be enjoyed.

I am old enough now to realize how many events in hindsight I did not fully understand or appreciate in my life. I am not talking about smelling roses along the way, though that is always good to do. It is not about enjoying the moments or gathering rosebuds while we may. We should enjoy every moment in life and soak up the good things along life's road. That is for another book and another time. Here, I am writing about taking a hard look at events, relationships, circumstances, and experiences to make sure we are doing well with them. I am also suggesting that, at some point, we should look down the road and wonder where these events, relationships, circumstances, and experiences might lead us. It is helpful if we can occasionally assess where we are and at least ask questions about where we are being led and what God might be up to.

As I have grown in my faith and watched others grow in theirs, I've come to see life is filled with potential and layers of meaning in the experiences of life that can easily be mistaken for coincidence or mere annoyance, especially by people whose faith has not matured. People of deep faith understand that God is up to something and has our best interests in mind. They understand that he orchestrates or allows us to experience things in which we might not see value. Whether perceived as good or bad, blessings or trials, they know that God is up to something with each experience he sends our way. It is their job to perceive it, enjoy it, decipher it, or just wonder at it. There is often more to our experiences than meets the eye, because they have value.

There is something odd about faith when it comes to sight. The Bible rightly says, "For we live by faith, not by sight" (2 Corinthians 5:7). What we see can be deceptive, but if our faith is securely in God, we are not deceived. In that sense, faith is much more reliable than sight. Faith is believing that what can't be seen with ordinary vision can be seen in other ways. The more firmly we trust in God, the more we know how much he can do, regardless of what our sight tells us.

Sight is mentioned in the context of faith in the Bible, but it is a different kind of sight. It is a way to see without eyes. Hebrews 11:26–27 states, when speaking purely about Moses' faith, that Moses was "looking ahead to his reward" and that he "saw him who is invisible." People have "eyes to see but do not see" (Ezekiel 12:2), if they are not walking by faith. The assumption is that there are those who do have eyes to see. One of the ironies in Scripture is that even though faith seems to be different than sight, they are often linked. Blind people receive sight when they encounter Jesus (Luke 18:40–43). Or they lose it and have it restored when they encounter Jesus (Acts 9:1–9), which happened with Saul on the road to Damascus.

Sight that is disconnected from faith is sight that looks at or near the events, relationships, circumstances, and experiences in our lives. It sees what can be clearly seen with human eyes and senses alone. Sight that is connected with faith is sight that looks through and beyond. It looks to God, who in turn allows us to look through and beyond our experiences to his shaping work in our lives. It is not that we cannot see what is before our eyes. We are just not focused solely upon those things. What we see with our physical eyes does not determine how we act or what we value, but what we see by faith influences and shapes us.

If we are going to know what God is doing to complete

us, it is important for us to believe that he is up to more than what we see in the events immediately before us. He is working through and beyond what we see and experience at any given moment. It is encouraging and enlightening when we have an idea of what God is doing to us and through us. We need to be thinking and looking at something other than what is happening in front of us. But how do we see what God might be up to that we might not otherwise be seeing with our physical senses?

The questions you ask during and after the events you experience that are out of the ordinary reveal whether you are looking only at and near or through and beyond. For instance, the laziest question of all is, "Why is this happening to me?" That question just seeks to cut to the chase and get an answer without thinking or pursuing the truth about God, life, or self. "Why is this happening to me?" is almost always a question asked when bad things happen, rarely when good things are happening. It is a self-focused question that implies that I am not happy. It is a self-absorbed question when I feel abused or neglected since it is usually asked when bad things occur. It unmasks that a person is generally airing a complaint rather than pursuing a truth. Rather than exploring what God might be up to, it is a question that seeks purely an answer to an isolated experience. Even if God were to answer the question, the person asking would not likely be able to understand given the emotion that generated the question. Habakkuk asked "Why me?" and got an earful of things he did not really want to hear (Habakkuk 1:2, 5–11; 2:2–20).

Faith-prompted questions dig a little deeper because they do not start with "Why me?" It is not about "me" per se, but about how God is fixing me, working through me, or allowing me to bring more glory to him. Eyes of faith allow us to see that God is up to something beyond what conventional sight or narrow-minded and self-centered sight will ever see. Here are some questions that help us to look through and beyond. The better questions are ones that look for reasons and for instruction that lead to change:

- What does this teach me about myself?

- What does this reveal about me and my character?

- Am I compromised or unsettled in my faith, patience, and hope because of this?

- Is my faith challenged by this?

- Is my hope intact despite the circumstances?

Those questions get us away from asking about the larger meaning of life that we might not really be interested in anyway in the heat of negative experiences. Unexpected events are good occasions to look at ourselves before we start looking for culprits to blame for our distress—God, satan, others, karma, fate, etc. Identifying culprits generally leads us on wild goose chases that never resolve anything. Even when we think we have figured it out, our conclusions are always debatable when we look for someone or something to blame for our distress.

The apostle Paul viewed chasing culprits as a meaningless activity. He told his own story of hardship and challenging experiences in 2 Corinthians 11:16–12:8. He graphically described being beaten, shipwrecked, robbed, flogged, stoned, hungry, thirsty, exposed, endangered by his own countrymen and foreigners alike, jailed, and alone at sea. Some of these things happened multiple times and in different places over a long period of time. He was making the point that if anyone had experienced trouble, he would be right there with them.

Theologians would be quick to recognize all four of the usual suspects responsible for the hardships mentioned in Paul's case. For the non-theologian, I will list the culprits responsible for our pain and suffering. They are *moral evil* (sin of the person suffering or someone else's sin impacting them); *natural evil* (volcanoes, hurricanes, and other natural disasters that happen in a fallen and imperfect world); *divine intervention* (God-ordained hardships, such as activities that we see particularly strong in the Old Testament famines, floods, and pestilences, for which God takes credit due to disobedience or evil in the world); and *satanic attack* (the devil or his emissaries who attacked Job, incited kings, and possessed people). Most people intuitively recognize these as the culprits behind human pain. They are the answer to the "Who is responsible for this?" question. These are the primary responsible parties for most of the bad circumstances that happen.

In Paul's narrative, he lumps everything together in those two short chapters in 2 Corinthians 11–12, without drawing much attention at all to them. He did not see the value of categorizing the responsible parties or giving a sermon about the role that the various culprits played in his misery. He spends little time whining about them, though by the time he had been hit hard by satan, we get the sense that he was pleading with God to take the problem itself away. I am sure he prayed during his distressing experiences. The one caused by satan stands out particularly forcefully in his telling of his story. Nevertheless, his conclusion and reason for telling this was not to blame anyone or complain about them or the experiences themselves.

Additionally, Paul did not feel it necessary (at least in his telling of his story) to talk about how God could let it all happen. We just see that people hurt him (moral evil); satan assaulted him (satanic attack); the elements plagued him through hunger, rivers, seas, etc. (natural evil); and a burden for the churches was placed upon him by God (divine initiative). He never categorized the culprits, condemned them, philosophically analyzed them, or regarded one above the other. He just noted that he experienced a lot of pain.

The culprit was of secondary importance. He did not even ask the common question of God: "Why are you allowing these things to assail me?" The big lesson was his focus. Through all his trials, Paul learned about God's grace, and he appropriated it. He learned some things about himself too, such as how his difficulties contributed to his own growth. These were his big takeaways (2 Corinthians 12:9-10). He discovered that God's grace was sufficient for his needs whatever the reason for it. He also discovered that it was in his weakness that strength had the opportunity to bud and grow. His conclusion was that God was at work in his struggle. He learned how he could become stronger with God's intervention on the helping side of life.

He learned a bunch about God and about himself when he did not spend his time asking, "Why me?" Or, "Who's to blame?" His focus was more on how to carry on the work of God's calling in his life, without unbearable weight dragging him down. It is not a question God entertains since he would prefer that we learn something of value and deepen in our faith. When people ask what they can learn, how they can grow, or how they can deal with the difficulties facing them, they are more likely to receive answers. After all, we can all grow and should be interested in that. Seeking to assign blame never matures us, but seeking to grow in faith always does.

Those are the questions that help us look through and beyond, rather than at or near. We look through a problem and beyond our circumstances to see how we can grow and develop. That is much more productive than looking at a problem and everything near it to see if there is a quick way out. When we look through a problem for growth opportunities, we are more open to having our weaknesses exposed. Paul discovered his weaknesses and grew as a result. When we discover our flaws and seek help to overcome our weaknesses, we are able to find God's grace and receive strength. If we understand that God really helps us in our weakness, then we can ask another set of important questions that are asked by those who look through and beyond:

- God, what do you want me to know about you?

- What does this situation tell me about your character and engagement with me?

- Is there a way I can hear, see, or believe in you better through this?

- How can the Holy Spirit help me in this trial?

These are not introspective questions to help us better understand ourselves. They are questions that help us understand more about God and how he works in a broken world.

It is hard for me to explain how this works. I just know that it does. God reveals himself very clearly to me when I seek him during difficulty rather than defending myself or blaming God for his apparent inattentiveness. Paul's lesson turned him from focusing on the problems to looking at them as opportunities for God to apply grace and strength in his otherwise weak and needy life. I have discovered the same for me. When I start asking God to use a circumstance to tell me more about myself and reveal more about him, meaning always becomes clearer. When I ask the right questions first, the answers to the bigger questions become clearer. The situation starts making a little more sense. Then the difficulty or challenge is no longer an annoyance or disruption to a perfect life, but a gift to help perfect my life.

There are still other questions that should enter in. We should not just ask what the circumstance tells us about our own character and what it tells us about God's character and presence. We should also ask God how particular circumstances affect others around us. Hearkening back to Paul, there were many people with him on his journey who witnessed and endured his struggles right alongside him. Others were looking at how he handled them. There were people who wanted him to crumble so they could swoop in and take his place. There were others who needed to see him thrive for their own survival. They needed to see his success and faith to bolster their own. The last chapter of Romans isn't something to gloss over in that regard. In it, Paul talks about the people who had helped him on his journey, those who benefitted from his partnership and those for whom he was forever grateful. Paul's experience ultimately benefited him and scores of others.

I do not know anyone whose life does not impact the lives of others. That's why we should realize that our struggles and challenges have significant consequences on others. Sometimes they are caused by others, often just as victimized or hurt as we are, perhaps even more. Sometimes those who observe our difficulties feel great pain. This is especially so for those of us who have had children who have been attacked, ill, hurt, or harmed in some way without our ability to contribute to a solution for them. Our lives are intertwined with theirs. Our pain becomes theirs. Their pain becomes ours.

People who look at a problem or near it rarely see those who are impacted downstream by hardships. They do not quickly see the residual pain caused by our poor responses to our circumstances. I have heard more than one person grieve over the pain they caused someone else due to their self-absorption during a time of personal crisis. I have also known people who have recovered from addiction or relational loss and used their experience for great gain and to inspire others.

Biblical history is filled with individuals who were able to look beyond. They looked beyond their difficulties to the prospects of helping others. Joseph demonstrated how to suffer for the benefit of family, friends, and even our persecutors. Joseph's brothers approached him in fear that he would seek vengeance against them for their betrayal of him. Surprisingly, however, he said to them, "You intended to harm me, but God intended it for good to accomplish what is now being done, the saving of many lives" (Genesis 50:20). The brothers were terrified because they were looking "at" the situation as it impacted them (Genesis 45:3; 50:21). Joseph looked "through" the pain to the many lives and nations that were delivered because of his experience, painful as it was.

David similarly made a commitment to King Saul, his personal enemy, by caring for Saul's family. Even though Saul sought David's death and destruction, David sought to use his circumstance to demonstrate his faith in God's deliverance and his own resolute commitment to those around him. That measure of commitment inspired the same in others (2 Samuel 23). The people who watched David's life exercised incredible courage and valor. The stories of their heroism are legendary. They were inspired by their proximity to David, who invited God to use each circumstance in his life to bring him to completion as a child of God.

I know leaders who have been heavily persecuted in a country that has threatened Christians and the church for many years. Their experiences have led them to expect pressure and even imprisonment for their faith. Government officials have taken possessions from them, restricted their mobility, and monitored their activities. They have made it difficult for them to live out their faith.

One of those leaders told me of his imprisonment by the police because they wanted to limit his Christian leadership and influence in society. He told me how they had put him in a prison cell block for nonviolent offenders. He mentioned to me that his imprisonment gave him the opportunity to share his faith with people from all walks of life. He said that had he not been imprisoned, he would have never met those people in need. God enabled him to share his faith with his captors and fellow prisoners alike. Many of them became Christians, believing in Jesus for their salvation.

The prison warden wanted nothing of revival in his prison. Silencing him was the reason he was put in prison, which became the warden's concern. This leader told me that he was reassigned to the most dangerous cell block in the prison, where all the hardened, violent criminals were held. After a few short weeks, revival broke out in that cell block as well. The warden was dismayed. He called the leader in to threaten him, but in the course of the conversation, the warden was convicted of his own sin and need for God. He believed because of that conversation. As a consequence of the warden's conversion and the transforming presence of God in the prison, the political leaders in that region of the country forced the Christian leader to leave the prison to keep him from bringing "the destruction of harmony" to their prison. Their desire to keep him out of prison outweighed their desire to keep him in it.

I celebrated with him that God had orchestrated his release. Interestingly he said to me, "I am never concerned about persecution or threats anymore. They are always opportunities for me to impact more people for the Lord. And God blesses our efforts with his grace even more when we are restricted. It is just another way and place to serve and help others who need God and deliverance."

I issue a warning here. There are many segments of the church around the world where what I share in this chapter is not embraced. Their teaching tells people not to look through and beyond their trials, but to pray for them to be eliminated immediately. All the energies of prayer and faith are to exercise disruptions or things that cause pain. The very notion of looking through and beyond the situation would equate to defeat in their eyes. Some believe that faith eliminates obstacles and does not grow through them as Paul told. The biggest problem with that approach is that lessons are never learned when the painful (but beneficial) growth opportunities are eradicated.

In my opinion, those theologies and segments of the church never find the blessings that God has for them. The larger questions are never answered, and their pain becomes increasingly unbearable when it is not eliminated every time. They have never learned to look through and beyond.

Praying for suffering to cease is good. Praying for pain to be removed is not bad. I pray often for it. But, for those who eagerly pray for God to remove the obstacles and pain but also have a higher goal in mind—the goal of discovering God's will and growing in their faith—God often removes the problem. But even if the problem persists, he always lends his grace. Like

Paul, we stand to gain a double benefit in times of need—God's grace and the lessons that can come only through experiencing weakness.

Project Me

- Consider a significant event in your life—something that you did not realize was so significant at the time. In hindsight, what made the event so significant? Why did you miss its significance at the time?

- Take a brief inventory of your life. What is happening right now? What is a major good or bad thing that's occurred? Do not ask God why it happened or is happening; rather, ask him how he can use you in the situation.

- Read Romans 15. Who do you know who has suffered for their pursuit of God's plan for their life? What do you admire about them the most?

10

Pray More and for More

I am an extrovert. I enjoy people and get energy from interacting and being in relationships. From my perspective, people are the most interesting and wonderful creatures in all of creation. Many people marvel at the sight of the Great Wall in China or the Taj Mahal in India or the Grand Canyon in the United States. I have seen them all and appreciate each for their beauty, grandeur, and design. But I find the stories of people unbelievably intriguing. How did they wind up doing what they are doing? Where are they doing it? How did they survive that tragedy? What led them to that life-changing decision?

Each person has a unique identity, personality, and experience. I love exploring that uniqueness. I relish opportunities to converse with people from all walks of life—rich and poor, majority and minority races, foreign and domestic, male and female, and young and old from every culture. Everyone has a story, and I find most of them fascinating, whether they see the fascination or not. Even when there are language challenges, I enjoy making an effort to capture the richness of a person's culture and experience. The only way to capture all of that is to have a conversation, and that's why I love them.

Having said that, I have been in conversations that are painful, forced, and difficult to sustain. I have ashamedly looked for the exit door of some conversations. Each conversation has an exit door, and I'm guilty of desperately looking for it on too many occasions. When conversations are forced by questions that never really prime the pump of interaction, they are hard to sustain, but conversations can be painful as well when the conversation is not really a conversation at all but a platform for someone to tell you everything about themselves with no interest in you or even engaging a response from those listening. When interest in a conversation wanes and one person disengages, it is time to abort. Some people are not self-aware enough to know when they are killing, dominating, or not participating in a conversation. When that happens, it becomes the other person's awkward responsibility to end it. And the question becomes how to conclude the conversation without offending. I do not think I am alone in both enjoying the right kind of conversation and wanting to end a bad one.

Enjoyable conversations are easy. They occur with people you know or with those you share an interest. They tend to have some interactive flow. A good conversation has a life—a beginning, middle, and end, complete with drama, sadness, and/or joy. They are unforced and have a healthy back and forth. They are vibrant, and any dead spaces in them are natural rather than awkward. There is no need to force topic changes; they just happen. When I am in a conversation that is going well, I hate to see it end. Time flies. It is not difficult at all to sustain, and it ends when it is time to end. We leave those conversations satisfied and looking forward to the next one.

The difference between good and bad conversations are obvious: They hinge on depth of relationship, shared interest, and interactive engagement (the back and forth of a good conversation). If you have a good relationship, the conversation has an advantage at the outset. If you have some shared interests, the conversation has a reason to exist. And if both parties are interactively engaged, instead of it being one-sided, it will be sustainable. Those are the ingredients of good conversations: relationship, interest, and engagement.

Prayer is conversation in its most intimate form. Talking to God, like all conversation, is not very good if there is not a meaningful relationship at the outset. The deities from other religious traditions are more conceptual than personal, making relationship with them impossible. In those cases, prayer is viewed very differently. They are not conversations but monologues, recited phrases, or repeated mantras instead of conversation. However, in Christianity, where we believe that God is not only a loving deity but also engaged in and among us through the Holy Spirit, we find ourselves in deep and meaningful relationship. Therefore, our prayer is based upon meaningful relationship and dependent upon our understanding that God created us and is deeply invested in us and our well-being. In that sense, prayer is relational at its core.

Prayer in this context also incorporates shared interest. God is interested in our lives and success. Likewise, we should be interested in God as well. God should receive glory for what he has created. We should be interested in giving him glory and honor for what he has done in creation and most personally with us. He has a vested interest in us. We have a desperate need for him. Both should matter to us. We exist to express our love and gratitude to him. Mutual interest and concern should exist between God and us. That makes our relationship the highest order of all relationships.

Prayer in the Christian context should also be based on engagement. God has engaged us through creation and the redemptive acts of Jesus Christ. He has engaged us through his Holy Spirit. He forgives us, loves us, and meets our needs. We thank him, plead with him, and seek wisdom and direction from him. That is genuine engagement.

Based on that criteria, prayer is our only way to conduct a conversation with God. It may seem a little more one-sided to us today than it seemed with prophets in the Old Testament when an actual, physical, or audible conversation with God happened with some frequency. But there is interaction in real prayer that should not be discounted. Anyone who knows how to listen well will certainly hear what God has to say. His conviction, comfort, and care speak louder than words.

We should eagerly seek engagement with God. After all, this is the most important relationship we will ever have. Ironically, while many people herald it as the most important activity, just a slim majority engages in prayer on a daily basis. In fact, according to a recent study by the Pew Research Center, 55 percent of Americans pray every day, and 45 percent say they rely on prayer heavily when making decisions (see pewforum.org/religious-landscape-study/frequency-of-prayer/). Similarly, the Barna Group found that 84 percent of Americans say they prayed in the past week. (They have been tracking that statistic since 1993; see barna.com/research/silent-solo-americans-pray/.) Many people believe in the importance of prayer and pray frequently. They believe it works.

In my unscientific interaction with people who pray, I find the amount of time most people spend in prayer is not very long. If we believe prayer is important, why do we pray only a few minutes per day? Why is prayer not sustained like a good conversation if it is deemed our most important form of conversation with the most important one with whom we can communicate?

The reason is found in understanding the full weight of what we've explored in this book thus far. Throughout Scripture, God is engaged in ways that exceeded the understanding of those with whom he was engaged. We've looked at how each event was more than a one-off activity. God uses and reuses each circumstance to build us, change the world around us, and impact people beyond our scope of immediate influence. We've seen time and again how impossible it is to fully understand everything God is up to. But he has proven to be up to more than we will ever know.

I have found in my conversations with people about prayer that most people pray for a single situation to be resolved, thinking that the single resolution is all there is. They pray for the healing to take place, the relationship to be restored, or the danger to go away. When the healing has taken place or has not taken place within an acceptable period of time, the prayer ceases. When the relationship is restored or worsens, the prayer is over. When the danger goes away or becomes more intense, the answer is thus interpreted and one can move on to other things.

Prayer becomes situational in this sense. It is either answered or remains unanswered by the deadline we have set; then the prayer may cease. There is a deep misunderstanding when the intent of prayer is approached this way—purely for visible and immediate answer. That approach allows no room for the answer to be other than expected or delayed beyond our expectation or found in a completely different way—for example, a personal transformation that resolves a situation rather than the situation being resolved directly. Prayer becomes less about conversation and more about making a series of requests.

If prayer is relational rather than situational, it should be progressive and more encompassing than praying for our individual concerns. We know that God is up to more than we can see. The answers may unfold over a period of weeks or months or years. In those cases, we should continue to pray. If we understand that God's time does not have an expiration date, we should keep praying until answer, clarity, or resolution is fully experienced. If prayer is a true conversation, then it shouldn't end as soon as we hear what we want to hear. Conversation with people we love does not work that way. We do not just approach them seeking an answer as we would from Google, namely getting the answer and walking away when we get it.

We seek answers. When we receive answers, especially from God, it spills over into a more detailed conversation about our perception on the matter of concern, thanking the person for the answers they provided. Conversing with God understands that spillover and contains gratitude, searches the deeper significance, and expresses deep thanks for God's love and reliability.

When we understand that prayer is more about the development of a relationship than an immediate answer, we pray longer and more often. When we view prayer as an endless desire to know God and understand his working in and through us, we pray longer and more often. When we are convinced that the work God is doing continues to unfold in new ways and impact the world around us in layers, we pray longer and more often. If we have growing faith in God, we will naturally pray longer and more often.

When we find ourselves involved in a lifelong and growing relationship with God, prayer takes on a different and more durable expression. Answers are unfolding all the time. When we think the answer has come, it may just be getting underway. When we think that no answer has come, we might find that the answer was a change in us or a redirection of our prayer to something else. When we understand *pleroma*, we know that God is going to do far more than whatever it is we are requesting of him. That makes us want to pray more and for more.

Praying more is what we should do. My family's personal prayers during the time Mitch struggled with cancer were rich. And we were not alone. That said, I noticed how differently people treat tragedy and relate to God in conversation because of it. When we learned our son had cancer, we prayed for his healing. It was the desire of our hearts. It is intuitively how all parents pray who love their children. It is the first response when people get bad news. We prayed fervently, and Marlene and I fasted. We prayed more than we usually pray, in fact. We prayed more deeply for Mitch than for anything in our lives before that. Again, I think perseverance kicks in when we discover our inability to bring about change by ourselves. If our loved ones are hurting, our prayer time and intensity increases.

We are not alone in this experience of intensified emotion and prayer. The Bible reveals increased intensity in stories with people who had similar experiences—especially in stories that involve losing a child. I've noticed that when an older person dies in the Bible, grief exists but there is not much depth or description to the grief experience. A few factual verses are all that was spoken about the death of greats like Abraham (Genesis 25:8–9), Moses (Deuteronomy 34:5–8), and David (1 Kings 2:10–11). These were great men, great heroes of the faith.

In contrast, the suffering or death of children is entirely different in the Bible. The narratives are longer. The grief is more intense. The weight in the words and emotions of parents and communities are heavy with pain, panic, pleading, and deep sorrow (see 1 Kings 17:7–24; 2 Kings 4:8–37; 2 Samuel 18:1–19:8; Luke 7:11–16; Mark 5:22–43; and Mark 7:25–30). Deep grief and desperation plagued the parents and the family. It was nothing like the anticipated pain and grief associated with losing one who has come to the normal time in life where we expect death and diminished health. Now, I am not minimizing the death or grief of anyone. I am just pointing out that, as one who has lost both a parent and a child, the nature of our grief in those situations is, generally, substantially different. Most children under most circumstances have not spent their entire lives caring for parents. But all parents have borne the responsibility of caring for their children. It is our responsibility and one of our deepest concerns.

That was borne out in our experience with our son. Our sense of urgency for Mitch's healing was much in line with what we see in Scripture. Our prayer life reflected our passionate desire that Mitch would be made well again to live out a full life with us. He had much for which to live. At only twenty-seven years old, he was engaged but had yet to marry. He was in full stride in his ministry as a youth leader. We prayed as parents often do that he would be spared. We even prayed that his pain would fall on us if healing did not happen. We lost sleep and our appetite, and we restricted our travel to be with him as much as possible.

Perhaps what surprised me most, however, was the different understanding and practice of prayer among some friends and church members as we walked through this experience. I realized that I did not know much about many of them. Some seemed to be exemplary models for us in prayer and supported and comforted us in powerful ways. It was as if their prayers and ours were the same and intersected. They seemed to form joint strands of prayer that were stronger than when we prayed alone. On the other hand, the prayers of some others were confusing and puzzling, like awkward conversations. They did not know what to say. When they did pray, it did not sound like something a person would say to anyone they really trusted with their lives. These individuals did not resonate with us as people who understood the character of the God to whom we were both praying.

We began our journey praying to God as we have experienced him through the years. We trusted God implicitly. We came with the presumption that God is good. We did not come with the expectation that if God did not give us what we wanted in the time and in the way we wanted it, that our view of him would diminish. We did not believe that his character or power were at stake. If anything, we believed we needed him to character any flaws in us through the experience. We did not enter the experience feeling that God was personally responsible for the pain we were experiencing. From our knowledge of God and relationship with him, we did not get the sense that God was inattentive or uncaring about our pain and grief. We never felt as though it was ours to give the ultimate, evaluative thumbs up or thumbs down on our view of God depending upon the outcome of this circumstance.

Faith shapes perspective. We believed in God at that time and that belief forms confidence. In this case, we did not believe that God was limited to one acceptable outcome with all other outcomes being unacceptable. We understood clearly that heaven is not a consolation prize or a punishment. Some apparently thought it was. We were equally clear that continuing here on earth a little longer, even if disabled, is not a failure either. We were surprised at how many people mark success and failure on the basis of how much pain will be experienced. Neither Marlene nor I felt as though our view of God's "performance" on this matter would be shaped by our pain quotient. Some who have shared our experience depart from faith. Others deepen in their faith. We relied so heavily upon God that deepening seemed our best and only reasonable option.

We assumed that God was at work in the present circumstance all the way through to the end. We believed God could heal, restore, and otherwise use this situation in countless ways for Mitch's growth, our faith development, and God's glory. We were convinced that God was up to something we did not fully understand. We knew things would be clearer on the other side of our experience, whether our prayers for Mitch's healing were answered or other answers we were praying against prevailed. We enjoyed praying with Mitch and had sweet times doing so. We prayed for him when we were not with him. We took time to have conversations with him, together with God, that were almost like group conversations where no one is quite sure who is being addressed at any given moment.

Our talking to God was prevalent some of the time; listening to him prevailed at other times. Sometimes he seemed silent; sometimes his presence and comfort were palatable. Sometimes the light would come on in our understanding of how God responds to us in our pain. We learned and deepened. At other times we complained, wondering why we prayed so often for the healing of others and had those prayers answered when with greater fervency and closer to home, it did not seem to have the same effect. God's involvement seemed a little arbitrary at times. We were certainly not perfect in praying, but the conversation continued. It morphed; it had ebbs and flows. There were moments of weary wordlessness. There were hours of ceaseless words. Still, the conversation continued, as did our faith and our sense of his love.

I found that we prayed more than we thought was possible over one situation. We prayed for over seventeen months, with one subject dominating much of our prayer, but we prayed for even more—more than we thought this situation was connected to. We prayed for the people impacted by Mitch's illness, for ways to communicate what God was doing in us, and for strength, wisdom, understanding, clarity, increased faith, confidence, and opportunity. We prayed for people undergoing difficulties with greater passion and understanding than we had before. We walked through the Scriptures with an increased understanding of how God resolves matters, responds to our prayers, and comforts. We also recognized how great the opportunities are when we have exhausted all our resources. We prayed more and for more.

For many who did not understand *pleroma*—the layers, the threads, and the ripples—how God redeems, restores and recycles, or how he works in time as we know it, prayer for Mitch was nothing more than a litmus test for God to prove himself. For others, their prayers were doubt-filled confessions intermingled with prayers for our son. It was prayer for a singular outcome that would determine a singular truth about God or their faith.

As a result, one very good friend sadly declared to me at Mitch's funeral, "I quit. Prayer did not work." When I heard him say that, my heart was heavy with sadness. I responded to him, "What do you mean prayer did not work?"

Prayer is not a manipulative mechanism to produce an outcome. It is a conversation that leads to multiple outcomes, all for our good and some that might take years to fully understand. Prayer is based on a relationship. Our relationship with God should not dissolve when we do not get what we want. It is based on shared interest on all matters. Do you really believe that God no longer has any interest in you? Has your interest in

God completely dissolved because of one matter? Prayer is also about engagement. Can you completely disengage from someone you have depended upon and from whom you have received a lifetime of grace? Can you do that in a single moment of disappointment? Jesus prayed in his last prayer that we would be with him in heaven (John 17:24). Still to this day, I find it odd that the fulfillment of Jesus' prayer can be viewed as a disappointment or failure. It just cannot be looked at that way.

If we are looking at prayer as a small and singular act, it will seem at times as though it works and at times that it does not work at all. To that man who approached me at the funeral, his prayer was for a single outcome, nothing more. The answer was his litmus test for believing in God. He gave God two choices and two only. His faith depended completely upon God's method of responding. If our prayer is more fully about the whole matter, how we live in and with it and how we relate with God and the world around us, then prayer is not just putting God to the test. If it is about our lives in and beyond our concern, then prayer will always seem to work since God is always up to something if we are just open to understanding what he is doing and have eyes to see it.

Prayer grows as we grow. Prayer expands when we understand how expansive God's work is. Prayer is not easily exhausted when we come to know that God's work is never exhausted. Prayer can only be ceaseless when we know that God never ceases to work in and for us.

It has been ten years since Mitch breathed his last breath with us, yet his presence has not diminished, and God's good work through his life is still very much alive. We have seen more than one answer to prayer. We have seen dozens. We have met people who have been transformed in countries across the globe by his blog posts and read the Scripture references he recommended. We have carried on countless meaningful conversations with people who received some answer because of Mitch's testimony. We have a better and deeper appreciation for relationships and family. Our communication is more thoughtful and deeper. Our prayer is more fervent and more expansive than ever before. The list goes on. Prayer works because God is always at work.

A persecuted Christian leader in a country where Christians are treated very poorly was imprisoned for his faith, separated from family, and treated very poorly by those who imprisoned him (who were of another faith). He told me that when he was placed in prison, his prayers were primarily for his release from prison. They were small prayers and based on his own desire. He told me that the longer he was in prison, the more he saw the needs of others and prayed for them instead. He was used by God to lead many to faith and help alleviate some of the pain and suffering in their lives. He told me that the longer he was in prison, the more his prayer changed. The more his prayer changed, the more he changed. And the more he changed, the more others around him changed. Then, when the authorities were ready to answer his prayer and release him, he asked them, "Could you delay this for two more weeks? My work in here is not yet done." His prayer has become more robust than when he was first imprisoned. Prayer grows as we grow. God continues his work in us and through us. Prayer is just part of that total work. It is part of the work we participate in as God does his work to complete us.

Project Me

- With whom do you love to have conversations? What is it about that person that makes you look forward to your next conversation? Is it your relationship, things you have in common, or just everything about them?

- Have a conversation with God. Talk to him about an important prayer that you may have given up on, whether you feel that it was answered or not. Take that situation to God in prayer. If it was answered, spend time praising God!

- Make it a goal to double your prayer time this week. God is longing to spend time with you and have extended conversations with you.

||

Be Thankful for the Clear and Unclear

If God has indeed begun a good work in us and is committed to carry it on to completion, then we should be confident that he is up to good all along the way. That means that he is at work in ways that we cannot presently see. It also means, as we have discovered, he does significantly more than we are able to see. He can remake, reshape, and repurpose our experiences many times over, and the ripples of impact will most likely outlive us. It also means that God uses our experiences in layers much more deeply and frequently than we will be able to ever fully understand. That means that others have benefited, or will benefit, from our experiences in greater ways than we can comprehend. If all of that is the case, how can we not be thankful? If God is doing so much, we simply must live our lives with gratitude for it all—for the seen and unseen, known and unknown, clear and unclear, realized and unrealized.

Thankfulness should emanate from our hearts, not just be a periodic activity. Most everyone gives thanks from time to time. "Thank you" is one of the most common expressions around the world. Every language has some way to express it. Traveling around the world, I have heard it spoken repeatedly and know how to say it in several languages: *gracias, merci, danka schön, xiexie, spasibo, maraming salamat, daniwad, asante,* and *obrigado* are some of the ones I use most often. Giving thanks translates into every culture. The best way to live, however, is not just to know the word, but to live in perpetual thanks. The redeemed should have no reason to live any other way. We should be continually thankful people.

There is a difference between giving thanks and being thankful. Everyone can drudge up something for which to give thanks. We see it on Thanksgiving Day. It is painful when a person must search deeply into the recesses of their mental calendar to find something or anything meaningful for which to give thanks. When it is trivial, it is often a humorous cover for the absence of something for which to truly give thanks. When the thanks is for something selfishly gained or for the injury of someone with whom there is disdain, it is disappointing at best and spitefully angry and sinful at worst. The expression of thanks is sometimes forced. It feels awkward to hear a person express thanks for something or to someone just to impress them. Giving thanks is an activity in which truly grateful people comfortably and eagerly offer while ungrateful people awkwardly or reluctantly conjure up.

Giving thanks is an activity; being thankful, on the other hand, is an orientation or a personal characteristic. It is tied to character. Living a life of gratitude is not dependent upon finding something for which to be thankful. It is a state of heart and mind. A grateful person has a thankful orientation. A truly grateful person might have a difficult time isolating just one, two, or even five things for which they are thankful. They live in a perpetual state of gratitude for virtually everything around them. And even in the most difficult experiences, they seem to find things for which to be thankful—tests to their patience, the gift of slowing down, the lessons learned when not getting what they want, an opportunity to live out their faith, the person who stood with them in a time of need, a deserved correction from a trusted friend, the comfort of the Holy Spirit in a time of difficulty, and, yes, the blessings along the way. The list goes on. The possibilities are endless for the grateful.

Paul noted that there is a secret to being content in every situation (Philippians 4:10–12). Contentment, like true gratitude, is not situationally dependent. Just as one can be content, whether they have very much or very little, one can be thankful for plenty or little. Grateful people find the nuggets or the possibilities for gratitude in just about everything. If they get what they want, they are thankful. If their desires are delayed, they assume there is something good in that as well. If their wishes are never fulfilled, they usually find better substitutes instead.

For the person who sees giving thanks only as an activity, their list of blessings is usually fairly short. It is generally limited to the hopeful or helpful—the things we have decided are good for us and work toward our benefit. For that person, it is easy to cull the bad and isolate a handful of qualifying good things for which to give thanks. And, when the list is finalized, it is generally small and limited to blessed experiences, gifts, or relationships. For the truly thankful person who lives in daily gratitude, it is very difficult to find qualifying things for which to give thanks. Everything that is not evil or destructive seems to qualify. Thus, it is a matter of unselecting things that do not qualify, a much more difficult task.

Being thankful is different than giving thanks. Anyone can do the latter. Very few are the former. Thankfulness should be considered a virtue. It is a virtue few possess but all can express it at least a little. Compare gratitude to love. Loving people love because love is in them. It does not need to be contrived or constructed. Their orientation is love. They would be called loving people by all who know them. They do not turn it on to impress or please a few select people. They genuinely love people that are both easy and difficult to love. We recognize them as loving.

Loving others is not a selective act reserved for those who meet their needs. That kind of deep and pervasive love is what Jesus said would change the world (John 3:16). It is what makes his disciples stand out as different from the rest of the world (John 13:34–35). Those who live in love live in God, because God is love.

Some people are loving to the core. Others have the capacity to love certain people and at select times. The latter know the feeling of love or at least the idea of love when it is expressed to them. They may not be loving to the core, but they have had the experience of being loved by someone and can express it to those people they value most. It is not a matter of being a religious or emotional person. It is inherently part of the image of God in which we were made. God is love. People who live in him live in love. They do not turn it on and off as though it were a spigot. People who are not known as loving people can express altruistic love from time to time, whether it is core to their character or not. They can give generously, meaningfully care for others, and demonstrate sacrificial commitment if the situation is right. However, that does not mean love is one of their core virtues rather than a periodic and select expression.

Loving people lean into love for all people. That is why Jesus would tell us to love one another as ourselves; in other words, love everyone. For loving people, loving everyone is not a stretch but a tendency. When Jesus spoke about love, he was not suggesting a selective activity where we only love people who are easy to love. He talked about it as a core virtue. He told us how we should respond to people regardless of what they deserve. He demonstrated what it meant to love everyone, whether they were easy to love or not. It was not dependent upon the one being loved, but the person doing the loving. In Jesus' case, it was not the lovability of the people around him but what was in him that made the difference.

Consider gratitude the same way. There are individuals who can periodically conjure up thanks for other people, experiences, and things. That is commonly done. We can all be thankful for that which pleases and satisfies us, but there is a much deeper experience for people who know that God is up to something marvelous. When a person comes to know that God not only forgives our sin and self-destructive behavior but can use our experiences in ways to help others, they are on the journey to having the virtue of gratitude. When a person knows that even death does not have the final word, they can be thankful through even the most difficult experience. When a person comes to learn that lesson, even in the worst kind of rejection, they know God will never leave or forsake them. Then they can be thankful for how God buoyed them through their most painful experience. When these things occur, gratitude will start taking over. It is embedded rather than contrived. It is not put on but put in.

Gratitude, in thankful people, is not just fueled by a sequence of events that trigger the gratitude. There is something much deeper. If gratitude were simply a response to a set of events for which we can give thanks, then it would be dependent upon the course of those events. In that case, if the events or circumstances are not favorable, why would we be thankful? We would be grateful as long as good things that deserved our gratitude were happening. When the good things would dry up, the gratitude would dry up. That is the experience of folks who see thanksgiving as a response to the world around them instead of a response to the God who has adopted us as his children.

Real gratitude, in the deepest, spiritual sense, is something that is within us. It is both a gift of God (as love is) and an orientation of life (knowing that God is always up to something for our benefit). Even when difficulties occur, there is a certainty that God will work it out in the end (Romans 8:28). There is good in our experience, or good is on its way because of our experience.

In Colossians 2:6–7, Paul said, "So then, just as you received Christ Jesus as Lord, continue to live in him, rooted and built up in him, strengthened in the faith as you were taught and over-flowing with thankfulness." I love the words, "overflowing with thankfulness." In these verses, Paul explains what growth looks like. To do so he employed a growth metaphor. He started using the metaphor of growth in chapter 1 when he spoke about grow-ing and bearing fruit. Here, he employs the growth metaphor again to explain how our life in Christ transforms from a seedling into a fruit-bearing tree. In these verses, he turns his attention to how we live with the knowledge of what Christ has done for us.

Paul was using a familiar metaphor for his readers. Receiv-ing Christ Jesus as Lord is the starting point. It is not just embrac-ing the idea of Jesus Christ but receiving him as our Lord. The metaphor of growth continues: The seed takes root and starts to grow or become established. We all know how critical the root is to the tree. Paul indicated that we cannot just "receive Jesus Christ as Lord" then discard him or ignore the implications of his Lordship. From seed to root, it is all about Jesus. He continued the idea from the seed and root and growth to being strength-ened. If we were to continue the metaphor further, the strength of a tree is its sturdy trunk and primary branches. Not surpris-ingly, faith is involved in our strengthening, just as it is in receiv-ing the seed. Faith becomes the operative work of the believer who accompanies and facilitates growth. Faith is necessary for us to see growth, and faith in the God who causes the growth is required for growth to continue.

Colossians 2:6–7 explains what a fully developed life of faith is like. The seed has taken root and grown. It has root, trunk, branches, and strength—all of which require faith from begin-ning to end. But the metaphor does not stop there. The fruit, as it were, is what overflows from all of that. It's the abundance of this kind of growth. And the fruit Paul refers to here is thankful-ness or gratitude. The natural fruit or overflow of a faith-filled life is an ongoing expression of gratitude ("overflowing with thank-fulness"). That is the bottom line. Faith is our response to God who causes the growth. And when we have faith in God and witness his working, we will most naturally be thankful. That is a key fruit element.

When we come to believe God is good all the time, gratitude accompanies all the virtues and acts like a virtue itself. However, where doubt prevails, gratitude does not stand a chance. Inner turmoil, suspicion, dissatisfaction, and worry will most likely win the day. In those circumstances, it is hard to be thankful for much. After all, the other shoe will likely fall. If something good happens, there is a good chance something bad will counter it shortly. The initial wonderful benefit becomes clouded by potential disappointment. When that is the case, how can the doubtful person possibly feel good about what is unclear? How can a person riddled with doubt be thankful for that which he or she does not understand? If it is difficult for doubters to be thankful for the good that is obvious, how much harder will it be for doubters to recognize and express gratitude for the blessings in their lives that are less apparent?

It's easy for most people to see and express their gratitude for the obvious blessings in their lives. They see something good and are thankful for it, and many people don't look any further. However, grateful people are thankful for both the clear and the unclear blessings. For the clear, it is easy; we see something good and are thankful for it. Anyone can do that. In fact, most people only do that. Grateful people look at the unclear and difficult to understand differently. If God is present in anything, they can be thankful for it. For the spiritually mature, this perception is as natural as breathing. From a faith perspective, we can be thankful for the good we see and the potential good that might be coming, which we cannot see.

1 Thessalonians 5:16–18 reminds us to "rejoice always, pray continually; give thanks in all circumstances." The words are in that order, which only makes sense. On the two ends is the charge to lean into joy and be thankful all the time. By faith, we know that God is up to good, always. By faith, we rejoice in what we have and what has yet to be given to us. That is the first

admonition. By faith, we give thanks in all circumstances since we know that each circumstance has the potential to lead us to good and to see God work. That is the final admonition. Rejoicing and gratitude sandwich the activity of prayer. They are the bookends, as it were, to prayer.

In the last chapter, we noted that people who believe God is up to something all the time for our good will pray with expectation. Here, we would add that being constantly in prayer can only occur when our prayer is fueled by joy and gratitude. Prayer that requires mustering strength to carry on a conversation with God is not sustainable. Prayer is only sustainable when there is an eagerness to pray. Eagerness to pray only exists in those who are faith-filled and lean into hope. Faith-filled people are by nature joy-filled and thankful. The only way to sustain prayer is to be joyful and thankful. When faith is sandwiched between underlying joy and thanksgiving, prayer naturally extends. It is not unimaginable to think of praying without ceasing as a possibility when we live in joy and gratitude. Living in joy and gratitude gives us constant reason to pray and a spirit that lifts us naturally into prayer daily. Expressions of gratitude become natural and prayerfully expressed.

Bob was nearly ninety years old. He always had a smile on his face. He greeted people at his church better than the official greeters. He was eager to ask people questions about their lives and tell a story about his. His face was not weathered from worry. He had embedded laugh lines and a smile that was well exercised. He never seemed to have a bad day. He was joyful. I am sure he had some rough patches in life. It is impossible to live that long without hiccups in plans or disappointments along the way, yet none of that emanated from his heart or countenance. When asked why he was always so joyful, he said, "The Bible says to always give thanks, and so I do (1 Thessalonians 5:18). More than sixty years ago I decided I would thank God every day at least a hundred times. I read that we should always give thanks and knew that there was much more for which to give thanks than I was doing."

Bob went on to tell that thanking God a hundred times every day was difficult when he was young. Now, however, he often surpasses that number early in the day. Why? He is grateful. There is no need to contrive thanks. It is the fruit of a grateful life.

Why does this matter? Why is it important to be grateful for the clear, unclear, and the questionable in life? Is this just another attempt to make optimism the attitude of choice? Is it so we can pump ourselves up when things do not go our way, making the disappointment look like a default success?

No! Gratitude should not be about staging or shallow optimism—rather, it should be about an orientation coming from faith. If we truly believe that God has started a work in us and will complete it as he promised, then our gratitude is not dependent upon momentary accomplishments or good gifts along the way. Those just fuel the fire of gratitude that is already burning. They will never start the fire. If blessings and favorable experiences are needed to start the fire of gratitude, then it will die out when the blessings evaporate. Thanking God for the clear is easy for the one who knows that God continues to work his way. Thanking God for the unclear should not be much more difficult for anyone who knows that God will work for the betterment of those who love him and are called according to his purpose (Romans 8:28).

Please do not get the impression that the unclear will someday become clear. That was not the experience of the kings and prophets in the Bible. The faithful described in Hebrews 11 did not realize the promises or fully understand the events in their lives. We should not be so smug as to think that somehow all the little ways God reaches out to us in the midst of our disappointments and hardships will make sense and become clear. They will not. But we should know that God is always making an effort to use it all to our benefit, and that knowledge alone should drive us to gratitude, even for what we perceive to be the unfulfilled or unclear things in life.

God is working an unbelievable work and deserves our praise and rejoicing. God will finish his work in us if we continue to trust in him and cling to him by faith with thanksgiving. That is reason enough for perpetual thanksgiving. When we have a thankful heart, praying endlessly is not a stretch—it's a natural outcome. That brings us back to rejoicing always, praying endlessly, and giving thanks in all circumstances.

Marlene and I are old enough to see how the pieces have begun to fall together for us and others we know. I cannot possibly count the number of times I have said or heard from others, "I did not know why that happened until now." Whether it was an unwanted move away from family, changing to a job that paid less, or a physical limitation, the reasons were discovered later in life. Even when our decisions were questioned by well-meaning friends and family, we would be thankful and continue if we knew the plans were God's. God is always vindicated when he is included. We will always be able to justify our gratitude when he has acted and completed his work.

So, if you are one who needs to change from giving thanks for the clearly beneficial to living a life of gratitude for all things rather than just the obvious blessings, you will need faith to get there. You will need to believe that Jesus did not die in vain and that God's promises are true. You absolutely must believe that he will complete the work he started in you. You must be convinced that he will do it well. You must trust that the pieces will make sense if you continue to walk by faith.

Project Me

- Compile a list of at least five things for which you are truly grateful to God (make certain these are qualified instances of thankfulness). Be creative, even being grateful for that unanswered prayer. Spend time thanking God for each item on your list by worshipping him and praising his name.

- Think of someone you have difficulty loving. List several good qualities about this person. Ask God to increase your ability to love this person.

- This chapter is about being grateful and showing gratitude, going a bit deeper with your thanks to God. Read 1 Thessalonians 5:16–18. Make an effort to thank God a hundred times today.

12

Expect More Than Self-Fulfillment

If everything noted thus far is true, then why are so many Christians filled with so much disappointment? If God is truly the one who starts and finishes us and has significant interest in our lives, then why do some feel as though their lives are without meaning? Since we are made in his image, why can't we trust him to finish or complete us? If we understand from personal experience that some of the most impactful and positively shaping experiences in our lives are not pleasant ones, why do we resist having them? If we concede that we will not know how all of it fits together until we are at or near the end of our life or in heaven, then why do we ask *why* so much? We know that we will not know the whole picture. If we have faith that God loves us and has a plan for our lives, then why do we try to craft our own plan and become frustrated or disappointed when those plans fail?

The reason is because many people do not think beyond self-fulfillment. That is the essence of it. If I do not feel as though life is becoming what I envisioned it, with the benefits I had hoped for, the whole enterprise is a waste. The desire to become who we want to be and do what we want to do is stronger than the desire or pull to become who God wants us to be and do what he wants us to do. Self-fulfillment has dreams and plans affixed to it with us at the center. Our plans are mapped out in our minds, and that is what we want most. Benchmarks are built into that. Expectations are tied to it. Goals are part of it. In fact, when I ask people around the world to tell me what they want their lives to become or reflect, they have at least a general idea. Most people have a very well-defined idea of what they want their life to be and reflect on what they would like to accomplish.

Regardless of culture, language, or race, people express their desires, which are, for the most part, noble. They want good health for them and those close to them. They do not believe anyone does their best when they are incapacitated. No one wants to live with debilitating illness, in constant pain, or watch their loved ones suffer either. People generally want to be financially secure and independent. They want their basic needs met and those of their family and loved ones. Most people do not desire to be rich or greedy, just satisfied. They do not want to spend all of their time and energy on survival. They want to have good and healthy relationships, loving and being loved by those close to them. No one wants relational brokenness for themselves or their loved ones. Most people would like to know that their life is making a difference in this world. They want to be employed in a job they love that has meaning. They want to be the best or, at least, very good at what they do for a living. They want to be understood. No one wants to live their lives being misunderstood or unappreciated. They want to be happy and enjoy life, conceding that everyone has difficulties. However, when they undergo difficulties, they want them to be minimal, making them more complete and aware of the reasons for the difficulties. In other words, most people want their life to make sense.

Nearly all my conversations with people about what they

want their lives to be or reflect include all or parts of those things for which I hope and yearn in my own life. I eat right, exercise, save for retirement, work diligently in my job, strive to have healthy relationships, and care for my loved ones. I try to minimize pain and suffering in me and others, the latter being an altruistic impulse. I want love, security, and significance like everyone else. I might add that if anyone is looking for me to denounce that narrative, I will not. Anyone wanting me to brand those as bad desires will be disappointed. In fact, they are all good. I can find some commandments, proverbs, words of Jesus, or instructions of Paul to reinforce these as good aims or pursuits. In some cases, I can even find strong endorsement throughout the Bible.

However, our hopes and dreams are compliments of something greater. They are not the greatest things but byproducts of the greatest thing. What is lacking in the narrative above? That description is primarily about self-fulfillment. Read through those desires again and I think you will find love and healthy concern in them. Altruism is there. None of them are unreasonable, and most of us, including me, would embrace them. But we should want more than that. Though these experiences, desires, and qualities are important, they must be part of a larger whole. They must be desires on the road to a grander destination. Our desires and hopes for our lives should be undergirded with two other elements: purely wanting what God wants (to will what he wills) and making an impact with our lives beyond what we can see and experience.

We should always seek and hope for what God wants to make of us and accomplish in and through us. That is higher than all of the hopes and dreams mentioned earlier. These good things are part of our humanity—fallen, redeemed, and restored. But for those of us who truly believe that God is higher and up to much more than we can see, it should be our desire to be part of what he is up to. We should understand that God expects more of us than our own self-fulfillment and satisfaction.

Our impulses lead us to desire good things for ourselves, our family, and friends. We want our lives to be meaningful and useful. We may even figure out how that is to happen and superimpose our wisdom upon God and expect him to flush out the good and meaningful in the way we believe it should be dispensed. That is where the rub exists. It is too easily assumed that we want what God wants—and in the same way he wants to accomplish it. We must resist that notion. God can do more with our raw material than we can. He knows what the good looks like at its best and how events in life complement one another. He better understands what meaningful and useful looks like beyond our dream. That is why we should want what God wants and will what he wills. We should not reverse it and just think that God should want what we want. He knows more and has the power to make more of our lives than our own self-realization. This is not a replacement of our desires but placing them before God and letting him deal with them. He will reshape them and give them surprising definition and meaning beyond our ability to fully understand.

Jesus did not just throw words together when he gave us a model prayer in the Sermon on the Mount. In fact, each word has meaning and reason for being in its place. Whole books have been written about it, and it is the subject of countless sermons. The Lord's Prayer has been prayed in thousands of languages for more than two millennia by billions of people.

In that prayer, Jesus started as all good prayers should begin: by acknowledging God and his place in this world and beyond what we see. Immediately following Jesus' acknowledgment of the Father, he offered orienting words for everything that follows in the prayer and in life below heaven—requests, confession, relationships. In the context of praying for God's kingdom to come and his will to be done, we acknowledge that the requests we make, confessions we offer, and relationships we develop are part of his will for us. We should be asking for God's kingdom to come and will to be done. That means we are praying for these fundamental matters to be dealt with as part of something much bigger than personal fulfillment. It means that in order for me to be fulfilled, there are other matters that need to be attended to first. I need to be forgiven. I need to be able to rise above perpetually succumbing to temptation and resist engaging in evil. I would like more than daily bread. I would like a stockpile of provisions for years to come. I would like God's forgiveness to not be contingent upon my willingness to forgive others.

There is not as clean of a break in that prayer as we may like between a cry for God's kingdom and will and the things we desire or need in life. Jesus did not pray for this higher order of things to occur (God's kingdom and will) followed by explanatory notes, commentary, or even a psalm-like *selah*, or tacit pause. He did not say something like, "I am praying first and foremost about God and his will. I will eventually get around to our basic needs and how we relate to people." The prayer is not long. The link between God's will and what we need are joined together by virtue of the prayer's brevity. Everything in the prayer flows from wanting God's kingdom and will to be manifested, presumably in us and in the world around us. What we desire can be very good. But if what we want is the sum total of our desire, we have cut the will of God out of our basic desires.

Our hopes and desires should be for more than self-fulfillment. We can get self-fulfillment from many different sources without ever getting God. But we cannot get God and be satisfied with self-fulfillment alone. We must know that our lives can be about much more than getting what we want. When our expectation is enlarged and our desires are expanded to want what God wants (his will being done), then something bigger overlays our essential desires. I am most fulfilled when I know that God's work in and through me is being fulfilled. When I am partnering with God, I will always land in a good place. However, when I have made my self-fulfillment my aim, I have abbreviated God's will to nothing more than meeting my needs.

I am not suggesting that I do not desire good for my children, to have my needs met, or to have healthy relationships. It means that I want those things because I believe they are part of God's will and desire for me. It means that if I do not get what I desire the way I desire it, I am alright. God will make it alright. I just need to know that somehow God is working his will in ways I cannot see. This does not mean the things I want in life are not good. It means that I think God is better and that he will supply the good things I desire in ways that are better and in accordance with his plan. The things I desire might not even look like what I want them to be. That doesn't mean that I am unloving; it means that I believe God's love surpasses mine and will be worked out in my life and the lives of those close to me regardless of the visible outcome

We can keep our good hopes and desires. We can pray for them. More fundamentally, we should want what God wants and desire to be who he wants us to be. We should expect more than what we typically want. Part of that expectation involves the pursuit of God and his will. We should want that supremely. The other stuff will come.

Jesus confirmed this higher desire in the same sermon and the same chapter where he taught us the marvelous Lord's Prayer. Matthew 6:33 has been called the Magna Carta of the Bible: "But, seek first his kingdom and righteousness, and all these things will be given to you as well." Our pursuit is not self-fulfillment or personal acclaim—it is God's kingdom and righteousness. We leave the results in his hands. We know, however, that he has our best interest in mind. He will make us into the person we should be. What then should we be hoping and looking for? To become the person God intended us to be, fulfillment is implied. However, the goal is never self-fulfillment in the sense that we become who we want to be unless that desire is what God wants us to become.

I do not pray as long or deeply as some of my good friends around the world. My wife, Marlene, my sister, Lynn, friends Tom and Sharon, pastors Moses Arwade and Shirish Ahaley, and my marvelous intercessor friends, Doug and Margie Newton, all pray in mature ways. When they pray, I feel as though I am involved in a healthy and very productive conversation with God. Time flies when they pray. I feel as though we are going to get somewhere and will see answers to prayer in miraculous ways. That has often and quickly happened after they have prayed. They are the kind of people that God seems to respond to in tangible ways more than others. I love to ride their coattails in prayer sessions. There are some similarities in the way they pray. I notice they are never in a hurry to get to the self-fulfillment parts of prayer. They will get there. They want good things as much as others do, but the prayer for those good things is likely to be altered by the time they get to them. There are many other things that precede the self-fulfillment part of their prayers. The more they pray about important matters of God's kingdom and will, the more the prayer for those desires seem to change, sometimes imperceptibly. They spend much more time seeking God, inquiring about his will and desire, listening for what God might have to say, and asking for their will to be aligned with God's. It is not as if they do not have things to pray about. They are not stalling for lack of requests. It is just that there are far more important matters to attend to than speaking hurriedly about what they want. Their joy seems to crescendo when they talk to God about his desire and will. Sometimes the actual requests seem small by the time they get to them. The desires are still there. They just become secondary to God's presence and will. They expect more than self-fulfillment. They yearn for God and his will and righteousness. Their prayer feels like it comes right from Matthew 6.

Another impulse for our lives should be making an impact beyond what we can see and experience. Even when we yearn for significance and for our lives to make a difference, it is generally with the understanding that you'll get to see the difference and experience the significance in the context of your family and friends. We should expect more than self-fulfillment that is limited to the range of our experience. God wants to use you beyond your ability to know how and where. Remember that none of the desires we long for are less than good, but they are limited in our thinking and to our experience. We can only see as far as our sight allows. We can only experience what touches us in some way. A world exists beyond our sight and experience. God is the God of that world too. He may have significant plans for our lives that extend to the world that he oversees, which is well beyond our personal experience and knowledge. We should want our lives to have meaning even where we will never know it or experience it. We should expect more. Our narrative should be bigger.

Chapters 1 through 8 in this book reminded us that God is up to more than we can see. The expectation of our impact should expand accordingly. The prophets and apostles did not have a clue how their words and works would be used and enlarged for centuries to come in places they had never visited and in languages they never knew existed. Imagine that. They were living and speaking and acting without a clue of the breadth and height and depth of their influence. Isaiah did not know that my heart would be touched in powerful ways when I read his prophetic words as a teenager. Paul did not know he would challenge me to pursue a holy life when I read what he wrote for the eyes of the Corinthians.

The same is true throughout history. I am sure that Justin Martyr and Polycarp were not aware how profoundly they would impact a young American pastor in the 1970s. I am absolutely certain that Augustine did not know how many people would learn from his wisdom and honest, personal struggles. Paschal probably did not think his wisdom would travel much beyond his life, a life that was cut short. John Wesley did not know how profoundly his conversion would impact mine. And I am confident that Charles Wesley did not have me in mind when he wrote "And Can It Be," which has brought me into deep, praise-filled worship on many occasions.

The same is true of the impact our personal contacts from the present have had on our lives. Pastors, friends, and neighbors have all impacted us in ways they do not know. They may have felt fulfilled or not, but, regardless, their words have stretched far beyond their lives. Their good deeds inspire others to duplicate them. Their acts of kindness have spilled over beyond the person for whom the kindness was intended. Some of them will go to their grave having little understanding of their profound impact upon others. One of my mentors is in heaven now. Bishop Elmer Parsons influenced me profoundly, yet, in his final years, he wondered if his life and impact traveled far.

This is true not only of present-day authors, teachers, pastors, friends, and family; it is also true of Bible characters and other historical figures. It can (and should) also be true of you and me. As good as the desires mentioned earlier are, there is more. Perhaps it is modesty that makes us blush at the possibilities. It may be true humility or just a lack of confidence. When I ask people, "What do you want your life to reflect? What do you want to accomplish in life?" far too often the answer starts with, "I just want ..." The "just" is limiting in itself. It is confined to personal achievements or modest and personal desires for self, family, and friends. We should not become proud, thinking that our influence might go viral. Still, God wants to do more, and you should expect more. You should pray beyond your visible world. Your part in the project of your own development is partly to ask God that the project not be completed until you have impacted innumerable people for him.

Betty Ellen Cox was a missionary from 1944 to 1979 in Central Africa. She went obediently into the mission field, although she didn't think she had "missionary skills." However, she was good with languages, and the Lord used her in that way. She created the only written dictionary and grammar language resources for Kinyarwanda and Kirundi that had been created up to that time. She did this to help teach nationals their own language and missionaries their newly adopted ministry language.

Betty Ellen also created materials to teach English to people from Burundi and Rwanda. These materials were created in the 1950s and 1960s and were among the few written language training resources of these once oral-only languages. Betty Ellen continued to provide these resources to missionaries long after her retirement, free of charge. Long after her retirement, beginning in 2005, a steady flow of African immigrants poured into the United States. People started searching online and found her materials. She was asked to provide these resources for use in schools and resettlement programs. She continued to provide them without cost. She did not want to profit from her lifelong labor of love. She was asked to provide these resources for use by World Relief—refugee camps, adoptive parents, ESL classes, and even Yale University have all used her language-learning materials.

When word got out that these materials were available, the Free Methodist Church posted them on their website and received more than 10,000 hits in a three-month period, with many visitors downloading the materials. They continue to serve as a resource for the countless refugees migrating to the West from Central Africa. Betty Ellen was long gone by the time the need was greatest for the materials she quietly wrote for a handful of missionaries and local African schools. I do not think she knew just how much she was participating with the Lord in his work of completing her. He had more than her self-fulfillment in mind, and she was delighted with that.

I have learned to take God seriously. He wants to use me for more than my own self-fulfillment. He wants to use you for more than your own fulfillment. I have had too many experiences where God has done more than I expected from a word or moment spent in someone's company than I imagined possible. I have learned to expand my expectations.

Project Me

- What do you want your life to look like? What are your goals?

- Match your goals to those that you feel God has for you. Are the goals you listed self-fulfilling? If so, work on your list so that they align more with what you feel God desires for you. If you are having difficulty with this action step, talk with a trusted accountability partner or your spouse.

- List a few people who have had an impact on your life. Do they know about this impact? Take time this week to tell them with a phone call, an email, or a letter.

PART 3 SUMMARY

We end where we began. God started a project in all who believe. If you believe in him, you can believe that he will complete it. He finishes well what he started. He fulfills his promises. He promised he would finish the project that you may not know needs finishing. God is up to more than we can see and experience. He is working on developing us. We are not passive bystanders. We look deeply into what God is doing when we look through and beyond our immediate circumstance to his will. We tend to pray more and for more when we know he is doing more than we can see. Gratitude courses through our veins when we know that God works beyond our sight, and we should expect more than self-fulfillment.

This book has addressed three basic ideas about making sense of our relationships and experiences. The first is that only God has the capacity to complete the project of our lives. He is quite good at it and has a plan that is much fuller than our plans. God is the one who started the work in creation, and he will finish the work in eternity. He is the one who saves us, and he is the one who perfects us.

The second idea is that the work he does is not always clear or discernable. We have limited understanding and never see the entire picture; thus, we must walk by faith, trusting that God is doing the work even when our experiences seem confusing or have little rhyme or reason. We must trust and have eyes opened wide enough to see what he is doing and thank him when he reveals it.

The third idea is that "completing project me" requires our full participation. It should go without saying that if we resist what God is doing and wants to do, it makes the project impossible to complete. Appeals to live by faith and obedience fill both the Old and New Testaments. There is a reason God expects our faith and commands our obedience.

We must understand that nowhere in this book or in the Bible itself do we get an assurance, explicit or implicit, that God is obligated to let us know why everything happens. Perhaps he knows we might be discouraged at the length of time he will take to get us where we need to be, or we might develop an inflated ego if we know we will be used greatly. God will make us into what we should be, not what we might want to be. His greatest work in us is to help us live according to his will and calling, not to make us feel fulfilled.

Who then should we be hoping and desiring to become? We should hope to become the person God intended us to be, allow him to shape us, and seek to understand how he is completing us and using us to impact the world beyond our full understanding. When that happens, we will know he is completing us. When we finish the race, the project will be truly complete. Let future generations be blessed.

Acknowledgments

The best place to start is at home. Everything I have done, everywhere I have served, and every effort I have invested in my development and the development of others has been with my wife, Marlene. She is part of the process of my completion, and I am forever indebted to her. We have had a marvelous partnership for forty-two years, in three countries and too many ministry contexts to count. Not surprisingly, our children Luke, Mitchell, Samuel, and Charese have lived out the best of everything I have written in this book. I have learned more from them than they have from me. Luke's leadership and constant pursuit of excellence, prodding others toward it; Mitchell's sage-like advice and absorbing and contagious love; Samuel's zest for life and aptitude for understanding people and cutting through the noise to that which matters; and Charese's unconditional love and tenacity for truth and grace—all have had a profound impact on me as their father.

I am also indebted to the friends whose prodding made this project happen. There are too many to mention, but those who read the book and offered advice, endorsement, encouragement, correction, or help along the way include Jerry Sittser, Larry Walkemeyer, Rob McKenna, Jo Anne Lyon, Steve Fitch, and

Ben Forsberg. They bless me in more ways than they know. Larry Roberts' and Jack Grady's constant prodding that I write down some of my experiences has always been in the background. My sister, Lynn, has modeled a life well-lived and generously invested in others. She served as a model for this work. My colleagues in ministry have made the journey enjoyable and offered many of the examples of kingdom living noted in the pages of this book.

Finally, and fully, I am grateful to the core for Jesus Christ and his incomparable love and sacrifice for me and the world. I would have nothing lasting, memorable, impactful, or important to say without him. I imagine that the writings of this book would be little more than wishful thinking if I did not know from personal experience that he can indeed finish whatever he starts.

About the Author

Matthew Thomas and his wife, Marlene, have lived in three countries and ministered on six continents and in more than thirty nations for over forty years. He has served as an educator, pastor, superintendent, bishop, overseer, missionary, college president, church planter, consultant, conference presenter, author, and strategist. He loves God and people, spending most of his time expressing it in official, and unofficial, capacities. His greatest passion is the pursuit of God and a life of holiness that honors him.

He wrote the book *Living and Telling the Good News* and numerous articles that have had a global distribution. His website, matthewathomas.net, includes his blog, updates on upcoming conferences, and his current writing projects. He is Lead Bishop of the Free Methodist Church USA and President of the Global Wesleyan Alliance.